Ancient Legends

❦ OF ❧

Ireland

Lady Wilde

Illustrated by Marlene Ekman

STERLING PUBLISHING CO., INC.
NEW YORK

Library of Congress Cataloging-in-Publication Data

Wilde, Lady, 1826–1896.
   Ancient legends of Ireland / Lady Wilde ; illustrated by Marlene
Ekman.
      p.   cm.
   Rev. ed. of: Irish cures, mystic charms, and superstitions. © 1991.
   "The material in this book has been compiled from Ancient legends,
mystic charms, & superstitions of Ireland and Ancient cures, charms,
and usages of Ireland, both by Lady Wilde. Compiled by Sheila Anne
Barry"—T.p. verso.
   Includes index.
   ISBN 0-8069-4888-4
    1. Folklore—Ireland.   2. Legends—Ireland.   3. Ireland—Social
life and customs.   1. Barry, Sheila Anne.   II. Wilde, Lady,
1826–1896. Ancient legends, mystic charms, and superstitions of
Ireland.   III. Wilde, Lady, 1826–1896. Ancient cures, charms, and
usages of Ireland.   IV. Wilde, Lady, 1826–1896. Irish cures, mystic
charms, and superstitions.   V. Title.
   GR153.5.W537   1996
   398'.09415—dc20   95-46295
                                              CIP

The material in this book has been compiled from *Ancient Legends,
Mystic Charms & Superstitions of Ireland* and *Ancient Cures, Charms,
and Usages of Ireland,* both by Lady Wilde.

Compiled by Sheila Anne Barry

10 9 8 7 6 5 4 3 2 1

Published by Sterling Publishing Company, Inc.
387 Park Avenue South, New York, N.Y. 10016
Compilation © 1996 by Sterling Publishing Co., Inc.
Illustrations © 1996 by Marlene Ekman
Distributed in Canada by Sterling Publishing
% Canadian Manda Group, One Atlantic Avenue, Suite 105
Toronto, Ontario, Canada M6K 3E7
Distributed in Great Britain and Europe by Cassell PLC
Wellington House, 125 Strand, London WC2R 0BB, England
Distributed in Australia by Capricorn Link (Australia) Pty Ltd.
P.O. Box 6651, Baulkham Hills, Business Centre, NSW 2153, Australia
Manufactured in the United States of America
All rights reserved

Sterling ISBN 0-8069-4888-4

Contents

Preface   5

1. **Witches**   7
    The Horned Women
    The Lady Witch
    The Dead Hand

2. **Fairy Tricks**   16
    The Dark Horseman
    The Cave Fairies
    The Changeling
    The Fairy Dance

3. **Fairy Vengeance**   31
    The Farmer Punished
    Fairy Justice
    Shaun-Mor

4. **Legends of the Dead**   40
    The Dance of the Dead
    The Stolen Bride
    Kathleen
    A Legend of Shark

5. **Legends of Animals**   50
    A Wolf Story
    The Phantom Horses
    The Monstrous Cats

6. Leprechauns and a Phouka 59
 The Leprechaun
 The Hidden Gold
 The Phouka

7. Magic Spells 68
 The Butter Mystery
 The Wicked Widow
 A Spell of Apples
 The Evil Eye
 The Legend of Ballytowtas Castle
 The Fenian Knights

8. The Power of Poets 89
 The Poet and the Farmer's Daughter
 The Poet's Malediction
 The Poet and the King
 Seanchan the Bard and the King of the Cats

9. Murder and Mayhem *102*
 St. Brendan's Well and the Murderer
 Sheela-na-Skean
 A Woman's Curse

10. Prophetess, Fakir, and Priest *111*
 Queen Maeve
 The Irish Fakir
 The Doom
 The Priest's Soul

Index *127*

PREFACE

THE three great sources of knowledge respecting the shrouded part of humanity are the language, the mythology, and the ancient monuments of a country.

From the language one learns the mental and social height to which a nation had reached at any given period in arts, habits, and civilization, with the relation of man to man, and to the material and visible world.

The mythology of a people reveals their relation to a spiritual and invisible world; while the early monuments are solemn and eternal symbols of religious faith—rituals of stone in cromlech, pillar, shrine and tower, temples and tombs.

The written word, or literature, comes last, the fullest and highest expression of the intellect and culture, and scientific progress of a nation.

The Irish race were never much indebted to the written word. The learned class, the ollamhs, dwelt apart and kept their knowledge sacred. The people therefore lived entirely upon the traditions of their forefathers, blended with the new doctrines taught by Christianity; so that the popular belief became, in time, an amalgam of the pagan myths and the Christian legend, and these two elements remain indissolubly united to this day. The world, in fact, is a volume, a serial rather, going on for six thousand years, but of which the Irish peasant has scarcely yet turned the first page.

The present work deals only with the mythology, or the fantastic creed of the Irish respecting the invisible world.

Amongst the educated classes in all nations, the belief in the supernatural, acting directly on life and constantly interfering with the natural course of human action, is soon dissipated and gradually disappears, for the knowledge of natural laws solves many mysteries that were once inexplicable; yet much remains unsolved, even to the philosopher, of the mystic relation between the material and the spiritual world. Whilst to the masses—the uneducated—who know nothing of the fixed eternal laws of nature, every phenomenon seems to result from the direct action of some nonhuman power, invisible though ever present; able to confer all benefits, yet implacable if offended, and therefore to be propitiated.

The superstition, then, of the Irish peasant is the instinctive belief in the existence of certain unseen agencies that influence all human life; and with the highly sensitive organization of their race, it is not wonderful that the people live habitually under the shadow and dread of invisible powers which, whether working for good or evil, are awful and mysterious to the uncultured mind that sees only the strange results produced by certain forces, but knows nothing of approximate causes.

Many of the Irish legends, superstitions, and ancient charms now collected were obtained chiefly from oral communications made by the peasantry themselves, either in Irish or in the Irish-English which preserves so much of the expressive idiom of the antique tongue.

These narrations were taken down by competent persons skilled in both languages, and as far as possible in the very words of the narrator; so that much of the primitive simplicity of the style has been retained, while the legends have a peculiar and special value as coming direct from the national heart.

Francesca Speranza Wilde

1.
WITCHES

The Horned Women

A RICH woman sat up late one night carding and preparing wool, while all the family and servants were asleep. Suddenly a knock was given at the door, and a voice called, "Open! Open!"

"Who is there?" said the woman of the house.

"I am the Witch of the One Horn," was answered.

The mistress, supposing that one of her neighbors had called and required assistance, opened the door, and a woman entered, having in her hand a pair of wool carders, and bearing a horn on her forehead, as if growing there. She sat down by the fire in silence, and began to card the wool with violent haste. Suddenly she paused and said aloud: "Where are the women? They delay too long."

Then a second knock came to the door, and a voice called as before, "Open! Open!"

The mistress felt herself constrained to rise and open to the call, and immediately a second witch entered, having two horns on her forehead, and in her hand a wheel for spinning the wool.

"Give me place," she said. "I am the Witch of the Two Horns," and she began to spin as quick as lightning.

And so the knocks went on, and the call was heard, and the witches entered, until at last twelve women sat round the fire—the first with one horn, the last with twelve horns. And they carded the thread, and turned their spinning wheels, and wound and wove, all singing together an ancient rhyme, but no word did they speak to the mistress of the house. Strange to hear, and frightful to look upon were these twelve women, with their horns and their wheels; and the mistress felt near to death, and she tried to rise that she might call for help, but she could not move, nor could she utter a word or a cry, for the spell of the witches was upon her.

Then one of them called to her in Irish, and said, "Rise, woman, and make us a cake."

The mistress searched for a vessel to bring water from the well

that she might mix the meal and make the cake, but she could find none. And they said to her, "Take a sieve and bring water in it."

And she took the sieve and went to the well; but the water poured from it, and she could fetch none for the cake, and she sat down by the well and wept.

Then a voice came by her and said, "Take yellow clay and moss and bind them together and plaster the sieve so that it will hold."

This she did, and the sieve held the water for the cake. And the voice said, "Return, and when thou comest to the north angle of the house, cry aloud three times and say, 'The mountain of the Fenian women and the sky over it is all on fire.' "

And she did so.

When the witches inside heard the call, a great and terrible cry broke from their lips and they rushed forth with wild lamentations and shrieks, and fled away to Slieve-namon, whence was their chief abode. But the Spirit of the Well bade the mistress of the house to enter and prepare her home against the enchantments of the witches if they returned again.

First, to break their spells, she sprinkled the water in which she had washed her child's feet (the feet-water) outside the door on the threshold; secondly, she took the cake, which the witches had made in her absence, of meal mixed with the blood drawn from the sleeping family. And she broke the cake in bits, and placed a bit in the mouth of each sleeper, and they were restored; and she took the cloth they had woven and placed it half in and half out of the chest with the padlock; and lastly, she secured the door with a great cross-beam fastened in the jambs, so that they could not enter. And having done these things she waited.

Not long were the witches in coming back, and they raged and called for vengeance.

"Open! Open!" they screamed. "Open, feet-water!"

"I cannot," said the feet-water, "I am scattered on the ground and my path is down to the Lough."

"Open, open, wood and tree and beam!" they cried to the door.

"I cannot," said the door, "for the beam is fixed in the jambs and I have no power to move."

"Open, open, cake that we have made and mingled with blood," they cried again.

"I cannot," said the cake, "for I am broken and bruised, and my blood is on the lips of the sleeping children."

Then the witches rushed through the air with great cries, and fled back to Slieve-namon, uttering strange curses on the Spirit of the Well, who had wished their ruin; but the woman and the house were left in peace, and a mantle dropped by one of the witches in her flight was kept hung up by the mistress as a sign of the night's awful contest; and this mantle was in possession of the same family from generation to generation for five hundred years after.

The Lady Witch

ABOUT a hundred years ago there lived a woman in Joyce County, of whom all the neighbors were afraid, for she had always plenty of money, though no one knew how she came by it. The best of eating and drinking went on at her house, chiefly at night—meat and fowls and Spanish wines in plenty for all comers, and when people asked how it all came, she laughed and said, "I have paid for it," but would tell them no more.

So the word went through the county that she had sold herself to the Evil One, and could have everything she wanted by merely wishing and willing, and because of her riches they called her "The Lady Witch."

She never went out but at night, and then always with a bridle and whip in her hand; and the sound of a horse galloping was heard often far on in the night along the roads near her house.

Then a strange story was whispered about, that if a young man drank of her Spanish wines at supper and afterwards fell asleep, she would throw the bridle over him and change him to a horse, and ride him all over the country, and whatever she touched with her whip became hers. Fowls, or butter, or wine, or the new-made cakes—she had but to wish and will and they were carried by spirit hands to her house, and laid in her larder. Then when the ride was done, and she had gathered all she wanted, she took the bridle off the young man, and he came back to his own shape and fell asleep; and when he awoke he had no knowledge of all that had happened, and the Lady Witch bade him come again and drink of her Spanish wines as often as it pleased him.

Now there was a fine brave young fellow in the neighborhood, and he determined to make out the truth of the story. So he often went back and forwards, and made friends with the Lady Witch, and sat down to talk to her, but always on the watch. And she took a great fancy to him and told him he must come to supper some night, and she would give him the best of everything, and he must taste her Spanish wine.

So she named the night, and he went gladly, for he was filled with curiosity. And when he arrived there was a beautiful supper laid, and plenty of wine to drink; and he ate and drank, but was cautious about the wine, and spilled it on the ground from his glass when her head was turned away. Then he pretended to be very sleepy.

She said, "My son, you are weary. Lie down there on the bench and sleep, for the night is far spent, and you are far from your home."

So he lay down as if he were quite dead with sleep, and closed his eyes, but watched her all the time.

And she came over in a little while and looked at him steadily, but he never stirred, only breathed the more heavily.

Then she went softly and took the bridle from the wall, and stole over to fling it over his head; but he started up, and, seizing the bridle, threw it over the woman, who was immediately changed into a spanking grey mare. And he led her out and jumped on her back and rode away as fast as the wind till he came to the forge.

"Ho, smith," he cried, "rise up and shoe my mare, for she is weary after the journey."

And the smith got up and did his work as he was bid, well and strong. Then the young man mounted again, and rode back like the wind to the house of the Witch. There he took off the bridle, and she immediately regained her own form, and sank down in a deep sleep.

But as the shoes had been put on at the forge without saying the proper form of words, they remained on her hands and feet, and no power on earth could remove them.

So she never rose from her bed again, and died not long after of grief and shame. And not one in the whole country would follow the coffin of the Lady Witch to the grave; and the bridle was burned with fire, and of all her riches nothing was left but a handful of ashes. This was flung to the four points of earth and the four winds of heaven, so the enchantment was broken and the power of the Evil One ended.

The Dead Hand

WITCHCRAFT is sometimes practiced by the people to produce butter in the churn, the most efficacious way being to stir the milk round with the hand of a dead man, newly taken from the churchyard; but whoever is suspected of this practice is looked upon with great horror and dread by the neighbors.

A woman of the mainland got married to a fine young fellow of one of the islands. She was a tall, dark woman who seldom spoke, and kept herself very close and reserved from everyone. But she minded her business; for she had always more butter to bring to market than anyone else, and could therefore undersell the other farmers' wives. Then strange rumors got about concerning her, and the people began to whisper among themselves that something was wrong, and that there was witchcraft in it, especially as it was known that whenever she churned she went into an inner room off the kitchen, shut the door close, and would allow no one to enter. So they determined to watch and find out the secret, and one day a girl from the neighborhood, when the woman was out, got in through a window and hid herself under the bed, waiting there patiently till the churning began.

At last in came the woman, and having carefully closed the door began her work with the milk, churning in the usual way without any strange doings that might seem to have magic in them. But presently she stopped, and going over to a box unlocked it, and from this receptacle, to the girl's horror, she drew forth the hand of a dead man, with which she stirred the milk round and round several times, going down on her knees and muttering an incantation all the while.

Seven times she stirred the milk with the dead hand, and seven times she went round the churn on her knees muttering some strange charm. After this she rose up and began to gather the butter from the churn with the dead hand, filling a pail with as much butter as the milk of ten cows. When the pail was quite full she dipped the dead hand three times in the milk, then dried it and put it back again in the box.

The girl, as soon as she could get away unperceived, fled in horror from the room, and spread the news amongst the people. At once a crowd gathered round the house with angry cries and threats to break open the door to search for the dead hand.

At last the woman appeared, calm and cold as usual, and told them they were taking a deal of trouble about nothing, for there was no dead hand in the house. However, the people rushed in and searched, but all they saw was a huge fire on the hearth, though the smell of burning flesh was distinctly perceptible, and by this they knew that she had burned the dead hand. Yet this did not save her from the vengeance of the neighbors. She was shunned by everyone; no one would eat with her, or drink with her, or talk to her, and after a while she and her husband quitted the island and were nevermore heard of.

However, after she left and the butter was brought to the market, all the people had their fair and equal rights again, of which the wicked witchcraft of the woman had defrauded them for so long, and there was great rejoicing in the island over the fall and punishment of the wicked witch of the dead hand.

2.
FAIRY TRICKS

The Dark Horseman

ONE day a fine, handsome young fellow, called Jemmy Nowlan, set off to walk to the fair at Slane, whither some cattle of his had been sent off for sale that same morning early. And he was dressed in his best clothes, spruce and neat; and not one in all the county round could equal Jemmy Nowlan for height, strength, or good looks. So he went along quite gay and merry in himself, till he came to a lonely bit of the road where never a soul was to be seen; but just then the sky became black-dark, as if thunder were in the air, and suddenly he heard the tramp of a horse behind him. On turning round he saw a very dark, elegant-looking gentleman, mounted on a black horse, riding swiftly towards him.

"Jemmy Nowlan," said the dark horseman, "I have been looking for you all along the road. Get up now, quickly, behind me, and I'll carry you in no time to the great fair of Slane; for, indeed, I am going there myself, and it would be very pleasant to have your company."

"Thank your honor kindly," said Jemmy; "but it's not for the likes of me to ride with your lordship; so I would rather walk, if it's pleasing to your honor; but thanks all the same."

Truth to tell, Jemmy in his own mind had a fear of the strange gentleman and his black horse, and distrusted them both, for had he not heard the people tell strange stories of how young men had been carried off by the fairies, and held prisoner by their enchantments down deep in the heart of the hill under the earth, where never a mortal could see them again or know their fate; and they were only allowed to come up and see their kindred on the nights the dead walked, and then they walked with them as they rose from the graves? So again he began to make his excuses, and meanwhile kept looking round for some path by which he could escape if possible.

"Come now," said the dark horseman, "this is all nonsense, Jemmy Nowlan; you really must come with me."

And with that he stooped down and touched him lightly on

the shoulder with his whip, and in an instant Jemmy found himself seated on the horse, and galloping away like the wind with the dark horseman; and they never stopped nor stayed till they came to a great castle in a wood, where a whole set of servants in green and gold were waiting on the steps to receive them. They were the smallest people Jemmy had ever seen in his life; but he made no remark, for they were very civil, and crowded round to know what they could do for him.

"Take him to a room and let him dress," said the gentleman, who appeared to own the castle. And in the room Jemmy found a beautiful suit of velvet, and a cap and feather. And when the little servants had dressed him they led him to the large hall that was all lit up and hung with garlands of flowers; and music and dancing were going on, and many lovely ladies were present, but not one in the hall was handsomer than Jemmy Nowlan in his velvet suit and cap and feather.

"Will you dance with me, Jemmy Nowlan?" said one lovely lady.

"No, Jemmy, you must dance with me," said another.

And they all fought for him, so he danced with them all, one after the other, the whole night through, till he was dead tired and longed to lie down and sleep.

"Take Jemmy Nowlan to his room, and put him to bed," said the gentleman to a red-haired man. "But first he must tell me a story."

"I have no story, your honour," said Jemmy, "for I am not book-learned; but I am very tired, let me lie down and sleep."

"Sleep, indeed," said the gentleman; "not if I can help it. Here, Davy," he called to the red-haired man, "take Jemmy Nowlan and put him out; he can tell no story. I will have no one here who can't tell me a story. Put him out, he is not worth his supper."

So the red-haired man thrust Jemmy out at the castle gate, and he was just settling himself to sleep on a bench outside, when three men came by bearing a coffin.

"Oho, Jemmy Nowlan," they said, "you are welcome. We just wanted a fourth man to carry the coffin."

And they made him get under it with them, and away they

marched over hedge and ditch, and field and bog, through briars and thorns, till they reached the old churchyard in the valley, and then they stopped.

"Who will dig a grave?" said one.

"Let us draw lots," said another.

And the lot fell on Jemmy. So they gave him a spade, and he worked and worked till the grave was dug broad and deep.

"This is not the right place at all for a grave," said the leader of the party when the grave was finished. "I'll have no one buried in this spot, for the bones of my father rest here."

So they had to take up the coffin again, and carry it on over field and bog till they reached another churchward, where Jemmy was obliged to dig a second grave; and when it was finished, the leader cried out, "Who shall we place in the coffin?"

And another voice answered, "We need draw no lots; lay Jemmy Nowlan in the coffin!"

And the men seized hold of him and tried to cast him to the ground. But Jemmy was strong and powerful, and fought them all. Still they would not let go their hold, though he dealt them such blows as would have killed any other men. And at last he felt faint, for he had no weapon to fight with, and his strength was going.

Then he saw that the leader carried a hazel switch in his hand, and he knew that a hazel switch brought luck; so he made a sudden spring and seized it, and whirled it three times round his head, and struck right and left at his assailants, when a strange and wondrous thing happened. The three men who were ready to kill him fell down at once to the ground, and remained there still as the dead. And the coffin stood white in the moonlight by itself, and no hand touched it, and no voice spoke.

But Jemmy never waited to look or think, for the fear of the men was on him, lest they should rise up again; so he fled away, still holding the hazel twig in his hand, and ran on over field and bog, through briars and thorns, till he found himself again at the castle gate. Then all the grand servants came out, and the little men, and they said, "You are welcome, Jemmy Nowlan. Come in—his lordship is waiting for you."

And they brought him to a room where the lord was lying on a velvet couch, and he said, "Now, young man, tell me a story, for no one in my castle is allowed to eat, drink, or sleep till they have related something wonderful that has happened to them."

"Then, my lord," said Jemmy, "I can tell you the most wonderful of stories, and very proud I am to be able to amuse your lordship."

So he told him the story of the three men and the coffin, and the lord was so pleased that he ordered the servants to bring the youth a fine supper, and the best of wine, and Jemmy ate like a prince from gold dishes, and drank from crystal cups, and had the best of everything; but after the supper he felt rather queer and dazed-like, and fell down on the ground asleep like one dead.

After that he knew nothing till he awoke next morning, and found himself lying under a haystack in his own field, and all his beautiful clothes were gone—the velvet suit and cap and feather that he had looked so handsome in at the dance, when all the fine ladies fell in love with him. Nothing was left to him of all the night's adventure save the hazel twig, which he still held firmly in his hand.

And a very sad and downhearted man was Jemmy Nowlan that day, especially when the herder came to tell him that none of the cattle were sold at the fair, for the men were waiting for the master, and wondering why he did not come to look after his money, while all the other farmers were selling their stock at the finest prices.

And Jemmy Nowlan has never yet made out why the fairies played him such a malicious and ill turn as to prevent him selling his cattle. But if ever again he meets that dark stranger on the black horse, he is determined to try the strength of his shillelagh on his head, were he ever such a grand man among the fairies. For at least he might have left him the velvet suit; and it was a shabby thing to take it away just when he couldn't help himself, and had fallen down from fair weakness and exhaustion after all the dancing, and the wine he drank at supper, when the lovely ladies poured it out for him with their little hands covered with jewels.

It was truly a bad and shabby trick, as Jemmy said to himself that May morning, when he stood up from under the hay-rick; and just shows us never to trust the fairies, for with all their sweet words and pleasant ways and bright red wine, they are full of malice and envy and deceit, and are always ready to ruin a poor fellow and then laugh at him, just for fun, and for the spite and jealousy they have against the human race.

The Cave Fairies

It is believed by many people that the cave fairies are the remnant of the ancient Tuatha-de-Dananns, who once ruled Ireland but were conquered by the Milesians.

These Tuatha were great necromancers, skilled in all magic, and excellent in all the arts as builders, poets, and musicians. At first the Milesians were going to destroy them utterly, but gradually were so fascinated and captivated by the gifts and power of the Tuatha that they allowed them to remain and to build forts, where they held high festival with music and singing and the chant of the bards. And the breed of horses they reared could not be surpassed in the world—fleet as the wind, with the arched neck and the broad chest and the quivering nostril, and the large eye that showed they were made of fire and flame, and not of dull, heavy earth. And the Tuatha made stables for them in the great caves of the hills, and they were shod with silver and had golden bridles, and never a slave was allowed to ride them. A splendid sight was the cavalcade of the Tuatha-de-Danann knights: seven-score steeds, each with a jewel on his forehead like a star, and seven-score horsemen, all the sons of kings, in their green mantles fringed with gold, and golden helmets on their head, and golden greaves on their limbs, and each knight having in his hand a golden spear.

And so they lived for a hundred years and more, for by their enchantments they could resist the power of death.

Now it happened that the king of Munster one day saw a beautiful girl bathing, and he loved her and made her his queen. And in all the land was no woman so lovely to look upon as the fair Edain, and the fame of her beauty came to the ears of the great and powerful chief and king of the Tuatha-de-Danann, Midar by name. So he disguised himself and went to the court of the king of Munster, as a wandering bard, that he might look on the beauty of Edain. And he challenged the king to a game of chess.

"Who is this man that I should play chess with him?" said the king.

"Try me," said the stranger; "you will find me a worthy foe."

Then the king said, "But the chessboard is in the queen's apartment, and I cannot disturb her."

However, when the queen heard that a stranger had challenged the king to chess, she sent her page in with the chessboard, and then came herself to greet the stranger. And Midar was so dazzled with her beauty, that he could not speak, he could only gaze on her. And the queen also seemed troubled, and after a time she left them alone.

"Now, what shall we play for?" asked the king.

"Let the conqueror name the reward," answered the stranger, "and whatever he desires let it be granted to him."

"Agreed," replied the monarch.

Then they played the game and the stranger won.

"What is your demand now?" cried the king. "I have given my word that whatever you name shall be yours."

"I demand the Lady Edain, the queen, as my reward," replied the stranger. "But I shall not ask you to give her up to me till this day year." And the stranger departed.

Now the king was utterly perplexed and confounded, but he took good note of the time, and on that night just a twelvemonth after, he made a great feast at Tara for all the princes, and he placed three lines of his chosen warriors all round the palace, and forbade any stranger to enter on pain of death. So all being secure, as he thought, he took his place at the feast with the beautiful Edain beside him, all glittering with jewels and a golden crown

on her head, and the revelry went on till midnight. Just then, to his horror, the king looked up, and there stood the stranger in the middle of the hall, but no one seemed to perceive him save only the king. He fixed his eyes on the queen, and coming towards her, he struck the golden harp he had in his hand and sang in a low sweet voice—

"O Edain, wilt thou come with me
To a wonderful palace that is mine?
White are the teeth there, and black the brows,
And crimson as the mead are the lips of the lovers.

"O woman, if thou comest to my proud people,
'Tis a golden crown shall circle thy head,
Thou shalt dwell by the sweet streams of my land,
And drink of the mead and wine in the arms of thy lover."

Then he gently put his arm round the queen's waist, and drew her up from her royal throne, and went forth with her through the midst of all the guests, none hindering, and the king himself was like one in a dream, and could neither speak nor move. But when he recovered himself, then he knew that the stranger was one of the fairy chiefs of the Tuatha-de-Danann who had carried off the beautiful Edain to his fairy mansion. So he sent round messengers to all the kings of Erin that they should destroy all the forts of the hated Tuatha race, and slay and kill and let none live till the queen, his young bride, was brought back to him. Still she came not. Then the king out of revenge ordered his men to block up all the stables where the royal horses of the Dananns were kept, that so they might die of hunger; but the horses were of noble blood, and no bars or bolts could hold them, and they broke through the bars and rushed out like the whirlwind, and spread all over the country. And the kings, when they saw the beauty of the horses, forgot all about the search for Queen Edain, and only strove how they could seize and hold as their own some of the fiery steeds with the silver hoofs and golden bridles. Then the king raged in his wrath, and sent for the chief of the Druids, and told him he should be put to death unless he discovered the place where the queen lay hid. So the Druid went over all Ireland,

and searched, and made spells with oghams, and at last, having carved four oghams on four wands of a hazel tree, it was revealed to him that deep down in a hill in the very center of Ireland, Queen Edain was hidden away in the enchanted palace of Midar the fairy chief.

Then the king gathered a great army, and they circled the hill, and dug down and down till they came to the very center; and just as they reached the gate of the fairy palace, Midar by his enchantments sent forth fifty beautiful women from the hillside, to distract the attention of the warriors, all so like the queen in form and features and dress that the king himself could not make out truly if his own wife were amongst them or not. But Edain, when she saw her husband so near her, was touched by love of him in her heart, and the power of the enchantment fell from her soul, and she came to him, and he lifted her up on his horse and kissed her tenderly, and brought her back safely to his royal palace of Tara, where they lived happily ever after.

But soon after, the power of the Tuatha-de-Danann was broken forever, and the remnant that was left took refuge in the caves where they exist to this day, and practice their magic, and work spells, and are safe from death until the judgment day.

The Changeling

ONE evening, a man was coming home late, and he passed a house where two women stood by a window, talking.

"I have left the dead child in the cradle as you bid me," said one woman, "and behold here is the other child. Take it and let me go." And she laid down an infant on a sheet by the window, who seemed in a secret sleep, and it was draped all in white.

"Wait," said the other, "till you have had some food, and then take it to the fairy queen, as I promised, in place of the dead child that we have laid in the cradle by the nurse. Wait also till the moon rises, and then you shall have the payment which I promised."

They then both turned from the window. Now the man saw that there was some devil's magic in it all. And when the women turned away he crept up close to the open window and put his hand in and seized the sleeping child and drew it out quietly without ever a sound. Then he made off as fast as he could to his own home, before the women could know anything about it, and handed the child to his mother's care. Now the mother was angry at first, but when he told her the story, she believed him, and put the baby to sleep—a lovely, beautiful boy with a face like an angel.

Next morning there was a great commotion in the village, for the news spread that the first-born son of the great lord of the place, a lovely, healthy child, died suddenly in the night, without ever having had a sign of sickness. When they looked at him in the morning, there he lay dead in his cradle, and he was shrunk and wizened like a little old man, and no beauty was seen on him anymore. So great lamentation was heard on all sides, and the whole country gathered to the wake. Amongst them came the young man who had carried off the child, and when he looked on the little wizened thing in the cradle he laughed. Now the parents were angry at his laughter, and wanted to turn him out.

But he said, "Wait, put down a good fire," and they did so.

Then he went over to the cradle and said to the hideous little creature, in a loud voice before all the people, "If you don't rise up this minute and leave the place, I will burn you on the fire; for I know right well who you are, and where you came from."

At once the child sat up and began to grin at him; and made a rush to the door to get away; but the man caught hold of it and threw it on the fire. And the moment it felt the heat it turned into a black kitten, and flew up the chimney and was seen no more.

Then the man sent word to his mother to bring the other child, who was found to be the true heir, the lord's own son. So there was great rejoicing, and the child grew up to be a great lord himself, and when his time came, he ruled well over the estate; and his descendants are living to this day, for all things prospered with him after he was saved from the fairies.

The Fairy Dance

THE following story is from the Irish, as told by a native of one of the Western Isles, where the primitive superstitions have still all the freshness of young life.

One evening late in November, which is the month when spirits have most power over all things, as the prettiest girl in all the island was going to the well for water, her foot slipped and she fell. It was an unlucky omen, and when she got up and looked round it seemed to her as if she were in a strange place, and all around her was changed as if by enchantment. But at some distance she saw a great crowd gathered round a blazing fire, and she was drawn slowly on towards them, till at last she stood in the very midst of the people; but they kept silence, looking fixedly at her. She was afraid, and tried to turn and leave them, but she could not. Then a beautiful youth, like a prince, with a red sash, and a golden band on his long yellow hair, came up and asked her to dance.

"It is a foolish thing of you, sir, to ask me to dance," she said, "when there is no music."

Then he lifted his hand and made a sign to the people, and instantly the sweetest music sounded near her and around her, and the young man took her hand, and they danced and danced till the moon and the stars went down, but she seemed like one floating on the air, and she forgot everything in the world except the dancing, and the sweet low music, and her beautiful partner.

At last the dancing ceased, and her partner thanked her, and invited her to supper with the company. Then she saw an opening in the ground, and a flight of steps, and the young man, who seemed to be the king amongst them all, led her down, followed by the whole company. At the end of the stairs they came upon a large hall, all bright and beautiful with gold and silver and lights; and the table was covered with everything good to eat, and wine was poured out in golden cups for them to drink. When

she sat down they all pressed her to eat the food and to drink the wine; and as she was weary after the dancing, she took the golden cup the prince handed to her, and raised it to her lips to drink. Just then, a man passed close to her, and whispered, "Eat no food, and drink no wine, or you will never reach your home again."

So she laid down the cup, and refused to drink. On this they were angry, and a great noise arose, and a fierce, dark man stood up, and said, "Whoever comes to us must drink with us."

And he seized her arm, and held the wine to her lips, so that she almost died of fright. But at that moment a red-haired man came up, and he took her by the hand and led her out.

"You are safe for this time," he said. "Take this herb, and hold it in your hand till you reach home, and no one can harm you." And he gave her a branch of a plant called the *Athair-Luss* (the ground ivy).*

This she took, and fled away along the sward in the dark night; but all the time she heard footsteps behind her in pursuit. At last she reached home and barred the door, and went to bed, when a great clamor arose outside, and voices were heard crying to her. "The power we had over you is gone through the magic of the herb; but wait—when you dance again to the music on the hill, you will stay with us forevermore, and none shall hinder."

However, she kept the magic branch safely, and the fairies never troubled her more; but it was long and long before the sound of the fairy music left her ears which she had danced to that November night on the hillside with her fairy lover.

*In ancient Egypt the ivy was sacred to Osiris, and a safeguard against evil.

3.
FAIRY
VENGEANCE

The Farmer Punished

THE fairies, with their free, joyous temperament and love of beauty and luxury, hold in great contempt the minor virtues of thrift and economy, and, above all things, abhor the close, hard, niggardly nature that spends grudgingly and never gives freely. Indeed, they seem to hold it as their peculiar mission to punish such people, and make them suffer for the sins of the hard heart and niggard hand, as may be seen by the following tale.

A farmer once lived near the Boyne, close to an old churchyard. He was very rich, and had crops and cattle, but was so hard and avaricious that the people hated him; for his habit was to get up very early in the morning and go out to the fields to watch that no one took a cabbage or a turnip, or got a cup of milk when the cows were being milked, for the love of God and the saints.

One morning, as he was out as usual by sunrise spying about the place, he heard a child crying bitterly, "Oh, mother, mother! I am hungry. Give me something, or I'll die."

"Hush, darling," said the mother, "though the hunger is on you, wait; for the farmer's cow will be milked presently, and I'll knock down the pail so the milk will be spilt upon the ground, and you can drink your fill."*

When the farmer heard this he sent a stout man to watch the girl that milked, and to tie the cow's feet that she should not kick. So that time no milk was spilled upon the ground.

Next morning he went out again by sunrise, and he heard the child crying more bitterly even than before.

"Mother, mother! I am hungry. Give me to eat."

"Wait, my child," said the mother. "The farmer's maid bakes cakes today, and I'll make the dish to fall just as she is carrying them from the griddle. So we shall have plenty to eat this time."

---

*The fairies have a right to whatever is spilt or falls upon the ground.

Then the farmer went home and locked up the meal, and said, "No cakes shall be baked today, not till the night."

But the cry of the child was in his ears, and he could not rest. So early in the morning he was out again, and bitter was the cry of the child as he passed the copse.

"Mother, mother!" it said, "I have had no milk, I have had no cake. Let me lay down my head on your breast and die."

"Wait," said the mother, "some one will die before you, my darling. Let the old man look to his son, for he will be killed in battle before many days are over; and then the curse will be lifted from the poor, and we shall have food in plenty."

But the farmer laughed. "There is no war in Ireland now," he said to himself. "How then can my son be killed in battle?" And he went home to his own house, and there in the courtyard was his son cleaning his spear and sharpening his arrows. He was a comely youth, tall and slender as a young oak tree, and his brown hair fell in long curls over his shoulders.

"Father," he said, "I am summoned by the king, for he is at war with the other kings. So give me the swiftest horse you have, for I must be off tonight to join the king's men. And see, I have my spears and arrows ready."

Now at that time in Ireland there were four great kings, and each of them had two deputies. And the king of Leinster made a great feast for the deputies, and to seven of them he gave a brooch of gold each, but to the eighth only a brooch of silver, for, he said, the man is not a prince like the others. Then the eighth deputy was angry, and he struck the king's page full in the face for handing him the brooch. On this all the knights sprang up and drew their swords, and some took one part and some another, and there was a great fight in the hall. And afterwards the four kings quarrelled, and the king of Leinster sent out messengers to bid all his people come to help him. So the farmer's son got the message as well as the others, and he made ready at once to join the battle with a proud heart for the sake of the king and a young man's love of adventure.

Then the farmer was filled with rage.

"This is the wicked work of the witch woman," he said; "but

as I would not give her the milk to spill, nor the cakes when baked, so I will not give her the life of my only son."

And he took large stones and built up great walls the height of a man, round a hut, and set a great stone at the top to close it, only leaving places for a vessel of food to be handed down. And he placed the lad within the hut.

"Now," he said, "the king shall not have him, nor the king's men. He is safe from the battle and the spears of the warriors."

So the next morning he rose up quite content, and was out at sunrise as usual; and as he walked by the churchyard, he heard the child laughing. And the mother said, "Child, you laugh by a grave. For the farmer's son will be laid in that ground before three days are over, and then the curse will be lifted from the poor. He would not let the milk be spilled, nor the cakes to be baked, but he cannot keep his son from death. The spell is on him for evil."

Then a voice said, "But his father has walled him round in a hut with strong walls, high as a man. How then can he die in battle?"

And the woman answered, "I climbed the hut last night and gave him nine stones, and bade him throw them one by one over his left shoulder, and each time a stone of the wall would fall down, till free space was left him to escape, and this he did; and before sunrise this morning he fled away, and has joined the king's army; but his grave is ready, and in three days he will be in this ground, for his doom is spoken."

When the farmer heard these words, he rushed like mad to the hut, and called his son by name; but no answer came. Then he climbed up and looked in through the hole at the top, but no sign of his son was there. And he wrung his hands in despair, and went home and spake no word, but sat moaning with his head buried in his hands.

And on the third day he heard the steps of men outside, and he rose up, for he knew they were bearing the body of his dead son to the door. And he went out to meet them, and there lay the corpse of the young man on the bier, pale and beautiful, struck through and through by a spear, even as he had died in battle.

And they laid him in the churchyard, just as the witch-woman had foretold, while all the people wept, for the young man was noble to look upon, and of a good and upright spirit.

But the father neither spoke nor wept. His mind was gone, and his heart was broken. And soon he lay down and died, unpitied by all; for he was hard and cruel in his life, and no man wept for him; and all the riches he had gathered by grinding down the poor melted away, and his race perished from the land, and his name was heard of no more, and no blessing rested on his memory.

Fairy Justice

The "red-haired man," although he is considered very unlucky in actual life, yet generally acts in the fairy world as the benevolent deus ex machina that saves and helps and rescues the unhappy mortal, who himself is quite helpless under the fairy spells.

There was a man in Shark Island who used to cross over to Boffin* to buy tobacco, but when the weather was too rough for the boat, his temper was as bad as the weather, and he used to beat his wife, and fling all the things about, so that no one could stand before him. One day a man came to him.

"What will you give me if I go over to Boffin," said he, "and bring you the tobacco?"

"I will give you nothing," said the other. "Whatever way you go, I can go also."

"Then come with me to the shore," said the first man, "and I'll show you how to get across; but as only one can go, you must go alone."

---

*The correct names for these islands are Innis-Erk (the Island of St. Erk) and Innis-bo-finn (the Island of the White Cow).

As they went down to the sea, they saw a great company of horsemen and ladies galloping along, with music and laughter.

"Spring up now on a horse and you will get across," said the first man.

So the other sprang up as he was told, and in an instant they all jumped right across the sea and landed at Boffin. Then he ran to buy the tobacco and was back again in a minute, and found all the same company by the seashore. He sprang again upon a horse and they all jumped right into the sea, but suddenly stopped midway between the two islands, where there was a great rock, and beyond this they could not force the horses to move. Then there was great disquietude amongst them, and they called a council.

"There is a mortal amongst us," they said. "Let us drown him."

And they carried the man up to the top of the rock and cast him down; and when he rose to the surface again they caught him by the hair, and cried—

"Drown him! Drown him! We have the power over life and death; he must be drowned."

And they were going to cast him down a second time, when a red-haired man pleaded for him, and carried him off with a strong hand safe to shore.

"Now," said he, "you are safe, but mind, the spirits are watching you, and if ever again you beat your poor good wife, and knock about the things at home just to torment her out of her life, you will die upon that rock as sure as fate." And he vanished.

So from that time forth the man was as meek as a mouse, for he was afraid; and whenever he went by the rock in his boat, he always stopped a minute, and said a little prayer for his wife with a "God bless her." And this kept away the evil, and they both lived together happily ever after to a great old age.

This is but a rude tale. Yet the moral is good, and the threat of retributive justice shows a laudable spirit of indignation on the part of the fairy race against the tyranny of man over the weaker vessel.

Shaun-Mor

THE islanders of Innis-Sark believe firmly in the existence of fairies who live in the caves by the sea—little men about the height of a sod of turf, who come out of the fissures of the rocks and are bright and merry, wearing green jackets and red caps; and ready enough to help any one they like, though often very malicious if offended or insulted.

There was an old man on the island called Shaun-Mor, who said that he had often travelled at night with the little men and carried their sacks for them; and in return they gave him strange fairy gifts and taught him the secret of power, so that he could always triumph over his enemies; and even as to the fairies, he was as wise as any of them, and could fight half a dozen of them together if he were so minded, and pitch them into the sea or strangle them with seaweed. So the fairies were angered at his pride and presumption, and determined to do him a malicious turn, just to amuse themselves when they were up for fun. So one night when he was returning home, he suddenly saw a great river between him and his house.

"How shall I get across now?" he cried aloud; and immediately an eagle came up to him.

"Don't cry, Shaun-Mor," said the eagle, "but get on my back and I'll carry you safely."

So Shaun-Mor mounted, and they flew right up ever so high, till at last the eagle tumbled him off by the side of a great mountain in a place he had never seen before.

"This is a bad trick you have played me," said Shaun; "tell me where I am now?"

"You are in the moon," said the eagle, "and get down the best way you can, for now I must be off; so good-bye. Mind you don't fall off the edge. Good-bye," and with that the eagle disappeared.

Just then a cleft in the rock opened, and out came a man as pale as the dead with a reaping-hook in his hand.

"What brings you here?" said he. "Only the dead come here,"

and he looked fixedly at Shaun-Mor so that he trembled like one already dying.

"Oh, your worship," he said, "I live far from here. Tell me how I am to get down, and help me, I beseech you."

"Ay, that I will," said the pale-faced man. "Here is the help I give you," and with that he gave him a blow with the reaping-hook, which tumbled Shaun right over the edge of the moon; and he fell and fell ever so far into the midst of a flock of geese, and the old gander that was leading stopped and eyed him.

"What are you doing here, Shaun-Mor?" said he. "I've often seen you down in Shark. What will your wife say when she hears of your being out so late at night, wandering about in this way. It is very disreputable, and no well brought up gander would do the like, much less a man; I am ashamed of you, Shaun-Mor."

"O your honor," said the poor man, "it is an evil turn of the evil witches, for they have done all this; but let me just get up on your back, and if your honor brings me safe to my own house I shall be forever grateful to every goose and gander in the world as long as I live."

"Well then, get up on my back," said the bird, fluttering its wings with a great clatter over Shaun; but he couldn't manage at all to get on its back, so he caught hold of one leg, and he and the gander went down and down till they came to the sea.

"Now let go," said the gander, "and find your way home the best way you can, for I have lost a great deal of time with you already, and must be away"; and he shook off Shaun-Mor, who dropped plump down into the sea, and when he was almost dead a great whale came sailing by, and flapped him all over with its fins. He knew no more till he opened his eyes lying on the grass in his own field by a great stone, and his wife was standing over him drenching him with a great pail of water.

And then he told his wife the whole story, which he said was true as gospel, but I don't think she believed a word of it, though she was afraid to let on the like to Shaun-Mor, who affirms to this day that it was all the work of the fairies, though wicked people might laugh and jeer and say he was drunk.

4.
LEGENDS OF
THE DEAD

The Dance of the Dead

It is especially dangerous to be out late on the last night of November, for it is the closing scene of the revels—the last night when the dead have leave to dance on the hill with the fairies, and after that they must all go back to their graves and lie in the chill, cold earth, without music or wine till the next November comes round, when they all spring up again in their shrouds and rush out into the moonlight with mad laughter.

One November night, a woman of Shark Island, coming home late at the hour of the dead, grew tired and sat down to rest, when presently a young man came up and talked to her.

"Wait a bit," he said, "and you will see the most beautiful dancing you ever looked on there by the side of the hill."

And she looked at him steadily. He was very pale, and seemed sad.

"Why are you so sad?" she asked, "and as pale as if you were dead?"

"Look well at me," he answered. "Do you not know me?"

"Yes, I know you now," she said. "You are young Brien that was drowned last year when out fishing. What are you here for?"

"Look," he said, "at the side of the hill and you will see why I am here."

And she looked, and saw a great company dancing to sweet music; and amongst them were all the dead who had died as long as she could remember—men, women, and children, all in white, and their faces were pale as the moonlight.

"Now," said the young man, "run for your life; for if once the fairies bring you into the dance you will never be able to leave them anymore."

But while they were talking, the fairies came up and danced round her in a circle, joining their hands. And she fell to the ground in a faint, and knew no more till she woke up in the morning in her own bed at home. And they all saw that her face was pale as the dead, and they knew that she had got the fairy-stroke. So the herb doctor was sent for, and every measure tried to save her, but without avail, for just as the moon rose that night, soft, low music was heard round the house, and when they looked at the woman she was dead.

The Stolen Bride

THIS story of Kern of Querin still lingers in the faithful, vivid Irish memory, and is often told by the peasants of Clare when they gather round the fire on the awful festival of Samhain, *or November Eve, when the dead walk, and the spirits of earth and air have power over mortals, whether for good or evil.*

About the year 1670 there was a fine young fellow living at a place called Querin, in the County Clare. He was brave and strong and rich, for he had his own land and his own house, and no one to lord it over him. He was called the Kern of Querin. And many a time he would go out alone to shoot the wild fowl at night along the lonely strand and sometimes cross over northward to the broad east strand, about two miles away, to find the wild geese.

One cold, frosty November Eve he was watching for them, crouched down behind the ruins of an old hut, when a loud splashing noise attracted his attention. "It is the wild geese," he thought, and raising his gun, awaited in death-like silence the approach of his victim.

But presently he saw a dark mass moving along the edge of the strand. And he knew there were no wild geese near him. So he watched and waited till the black mass came closer, and then he distinctly perceived four stout men carrying a bier on their shoul-

ders, on which lay a corpse covered with a white cloth. For a few moments they laid it down, apparently to rest themselves, and the Kern instantly fired; on which the four men ran away shrieking, and the corpse was left alone on the bier. Kern of Querin immediately sprang to the place and, lifting the cloth from the face of the corpse, beheld by the freezing starlight, the form of a beautiful young girl, apparently not dead but in a deep sleep.

Gently he passed his hand over her face and raised her up, when she opened her eyes and looked around with wild wonder, but spake never a word, though he tried to soothe and encourage her. Then, thinking it was dangerous for them to remain in that place, he raised her from the bier, and taking her hand led her away to his own house. They arrived safely, but in silence. And for twelve months did she remain with the Kern, never tasting food or speaking a word for all that time.

When the next November Eve came round, he resolved to visit the east strand again, and watch from the same place, in the hope of meeting with some adventure that might throw light on the history of the beautiful girl. His way lay beside the old ruined fort called *Lios-na-fallainge* (the Fort of the Mantle), and as he passed, the sound of music and mirth fell on his ear. He stopped to catch the words of the voices, and had not waited long when he heard a man say in a low whisper, "Where shall we go tonight to carry off a bride?"

And a second voice answered, "Wherever we go I hope better luck will be ours than we had this day twelvemonths."

"Yes," said a third, "on that night we carried off a rich prize, the fair daughter of O'Connor; but that clown, the Kern of Querin, broke our spell and took her from us. Yet little pleasure has he had of his bride, for she has neither eaten nor drank nor uttered a word since she entered his house."

"And so she will remain," said a fourth, "until he makes her eat off her father's tablecloth, which covered her as she lay on the bier, and which is now thrown up over the top of her bed."

On hearing all this, the Kern rushed home, and without waiting even for the morning, entered the young girl's room, took down the tablecloth, spread it on the table, laid meat and drink thereon, and led her to it. "Drink," he said, "that speech may come to you." And she drank, and ate of the food, and then speech came. And she told the Kern her story—how she was to have been married to a young lord of her own country, and the wedding guests had all assembled, when she felt herself suddenly ill and swooned away, and never knew more of what had happened to her until the Kern had passed his hand over her face, by which she recovered consciousness, but could neither eat nor speak, for a spell was on her, and she was helpless.

Then the Kern prepared a chariot, and carried home the young girl to her father, who was like to die for joy when he beheld her. And the Kern grew mightily in O'Connor's favor, so that at last he gave him his fair young daughter to wife; and the wedded pair lived together happily for many long years after, and no evil befell them, but good followed all the work of their hands.

Kathleen

A young girl from Innis-Sark had a lover, a fine young fellow, who met his death by an accident, to her great grief and sorrow. One evening at sunset, as she sat by the roadside crying her eyes out, a beautiful lady came by, all in white, and tapped her on the cheek.

"Don't cry, Kathleen," she said, "your lover is safe. Just take this ring of herbs and look through it and you will see him. He is with a grand company, and wears a golden circlet on his head and a scarlet sash round his waist."

So Kathleen took the ring of herbs and looked through it, and there indeed was her lover in the midst of a great company dancing on the hill; and he was very pale, but handsomer than ever, with the gold circlet round his head, as if they had made him a prince.

"Now," said the lady, "here is a larger ring of herbs. Take it, and whenever you want to see your lover, pluck a leaf from it and burn it; and a great smoke will arise, and you will fall into a trance; and in the trance your lover will carry you away to the fairy rath, and there you may dance all night with him on the greensward. But say no prayer, and make no sign of the cross while the smoke is rising, or your lover will disappear forever."

From that time a great change came over Kathleen. She said no prayer, and cared for no priest, and never made the sign of the cross, but every night shut herself up in her room, and burned a leaf of the ring of herbs as she had been told; and when the smoke arose she fell into a deep sleep and knew no more. But in the morning she told her people that, though she seemed to be lying in her bed, she was far away with the fairies on the hill dancing with her lover. And she was very happy in her new life, and wanted no priest nor prayer nor mass anymore, and all the dead were there dancing with the rest, all the people she had known; and they welcomed her and gave her wine to drink in little crystal cups, and told her she must soon come and stay with them and with her lover forevermore.

Now Kathleen's mother was a good, honest, religious woman, and she fretted much over her daughter's strange state, for she knew the girl had been fairy-struck. So she determined to watch; and one night when Kathleen went to her bed as usual all alone by herself in the room, for she would allow no one to be with her, the mother crept up and looked through a chink in the door, and then she saw Kathleen take the round ring of herbs from a secret place in the press and pluck a leaf from it and burn it, on which a great smoke arose and the girl fell on her bed in a deep trance.

Now the mother could no longer keep silence, for she saw there was devil's work in it; and she fell on her knees and prayed aloud "Oh Maia, mother, send the evil spirit away from the child!" And she rushed into the room and made the sign of the cross over the sleeping girl, when immediately Kathleen started up and screamed, "Mother! mother! the dead are coming for me! They are here! They are here!"

And her features looked like one in a fit. Then the poor mother sent for the priest, who came at once, and threw holy water on the girl, and said prayers over her; and he took the ring of herbs that lay beside her and cursed it forevermore, and instantly it fell to powder and lay like grey ashes on the floor. After this Kathleen grew calmer, and the evil spirit seemed to have left her, but she was too weak to move or to speak, or to utter a prayer, and before the clock struck twelve that night she lay dead.

A Legend of Shark

On Shark Island there lived some years ago a woman named Mary Callan, with her one only child. Indeed, she never had another, from the fright she got some weeks after her baby was born, and this was her strange story. Suddenly, at dead of night, she was awoke by the child crying, and starting up, she lit the candle, when to her horror she saw two strange men standing beside her bed, and they threw a mantle over her and drew her out of the house into the dark night; and there at the door she saw a horse waiting, and one of them lifted her up, and then sprang up himself, and they rode away like the wind into the darkness.

Presently they came to a great, black-looking house, where a woman was waiting, who brought her in, and she found herself all at once in a splendid hall lit up with torches and hung with silk. And the woman told her to sit down and wait till she was called, as there was very important business for her to attend to. Now, when the woman left her alone, Mary began to look about her with great curiosity, and a large silver pot on the table, filled with sweet-smelling ointment, especially attracted her, so that she could not help rubbing some on her hands, and touched her eyes with the fragrant salve.

Then suddenly a strange thing happened, for the room seemed filled with children, but she knew that they were all dead, for some of them were from her own village, and she remembered their names, and when they died.

As she watched them, one of the children came over quite close, and looking fixedly at her, asked: "What brought you here, Mary, to this dreadful place? For no one can leave it until the Judgment Day, and we dwell for ever in sorrow for the life that has been taken from us. And the men went for your child to-night, to bring it here amongst the dead, but when you struck a light they could do no harm; yet they are still watching for it, so hasten back, or it will be too late, and the child will die. And tell my mother that I am with the spirits of the hill, and not to fret, for we shall meet again on the Judgment Day."

"But how can I go out in the darkness?" asked Mary, "for I know not my way."

"Never mind," said the child. "Here, take this leaf, and crush it close in your hand, and it will guide you safe from harm."

And she placed a green leaf in the woman's hand, and on the instant Mary found herself outside the door of the great house; but a tremor fell on her, for loud voices were heard calling her back, and footsteps seemed to pursue her as she fled away. Then, just as she was sinking to the earth with fright, she grasped the leaf close in her hand, and in a moment she was at her own door, and the footsteps of the pursuers ceased; but she heard a great cry within the house, and a woman rushed out and seized her arm. "Come, Mary," she said, "come quickly. Your child is dying. Something is strangling it, and we cannot help or save him."

Then Mary, wild with fear, sprang to the little bed where lay the child, and he was quite black in the face, as if someone was holding him by the throat; but, quick as thought, Mary took the leaf and crushed it into the child's hand. And gradually the convulsion passed away, and the natural color came back, and in a little while he slept peacefully in his mother's arms, and she laid him in his bed and watched by him all night; but no harm came, and no evil thing touched him. And in the morning he smiled up at his mother, bright and rosy as ever, and then she knew that the fairy power was broken, and the child was saved by the spell of the leaf that had come to her from the hands of the dead that dwell in the Spirit Land. And Mary made a case for the leaf, and worked it richly, and tied it round her neck to wear forevermore. And from that day the fairies ceased to molest her, and her child grew and prospered, for the spirits of the dead watched over him to keep him safe from harm.

5.
LEGENDS OF
ANIMALS

A Wolf Story

Transformation into wolves is a favorite subject of Irish legend, and many a wild tale is told by the peasants round the turf fire in the winter nights of strange adventures with wolves. These stories had come down to them from their forefathers in the old times long ago. In those days, the wolves in Ireland had increased to such an extent, owing to the desolation of the country by constant wars, that a reward was offered and a high price paid for every wolf's skin brought into the court of the justiciary; and this was in the time of Queen Elizabeth, when the English troops made ceaseless war against the Irish people, and there were more wolves in Ireland than men; and the dead lay unburied in hundreds on the highways, for there were no hands left to dig them graves. There are no wolves existing now in Ireland.

A young farmer named Connor once missed two fine cows from his herd, and no tale or tidings could be heard of them anywhere. So he thought he would set out on a search throughout the country; and he took a stout blackthorn stick in his hand, and went his way. All day he travelled miles and miles, but never a sign of the cattle. And the evening began to grow very dark, and he was wearied and hungry, and no place near to rest in; for he was in the midst of a bleak, desolate heath, with never a habitation at all in sight, except a long, low, rude shieling, like the den of a robber or a wild beast. But a gleam of light came from a chink between the boards, and Connor took heart and went up and knocked at the door. It was opened at once by a tall, thin, grey-haired old man, with keen, dark eyes.

"Come in," he said, "you are welcome. We have been waiting for you. This is my wife," and he brought him over to the hearth, where was seated an old, thin, grey woman, with long, sharp teeth and terrible glittering eyes.

"You are welcome," she said. "We have been waiting for you—it is time for supper. Sit down and eat with us."

Now Connor was a brave fellow, but he was a little dazed at

first at the sight of this strange creature. However, as he had his stout stick with him, he thought he could make a fight for his life anyway, and, meantime, he would rest and eat, for he was both hungry and weary, and it was now black night, and he would never find his way home even if he tried. So he sat down by the hearth, while the old grey woman stirred the pot on the fire. But Connor felt that she was watching him all the time with her keen, sharp eyes.

Then a knock came to the door. And the old man rose up and opened it. In walked a slender, young black wolf, who went straight across to an inner room, from which in a few moments came forth a dark, slender, handsome youth, who took his place at the table and looked hard at Connor with his glittering eyes.

"You are welcome," he said, "we have waited for you."

Before Connor could answer, another knock was heard, and in came a second wolf, who passed on to the inner room like the first, and soon after, another dark, handsome youth came out and sat down to supper, glaring at Connor with his keen eyes.

"These are our sons," said the old man. "Tell them what you want, and what brought you here amongst us, for we live alone and don't care to have spies and strangers coming to our place."

Then Connor told his story, how he had lost his two fine cows, and had searched all day and found no trace of them; and he knew nothing of the place he was in, nor of the kindly gentleman who asked him to supper; but if they just told him where to find his cows he would thank them, and make his way home.

Then they all laughed and looked at each other, and the old hag looked more frightful than ever when she showed her long, sharp teeth.

On this, Connor grew angry, for he was hot-tempered; and he grasped his blackthorn stick firmly in his hand and stood up, and bade them open the door for him; for he would go his way, since they would give no heed and only mocked him.

Then the eldest of the young men stood up. "Wait," he said, "we are fierce and evil, but we never forget a kindness. Do you remember, one day down in the glen you found a poor little wolf in great agony and like to die, because a sharp thorn had pierced

his side? And you gently extracted the thorn and gave him a drink, and went your way leaving him in peace and rest?"

"Aye, well do I remember it," said Connor, "and how the poor little beast licked my hand in gratitude."

"Well," said the young man, "I am that wolf, and I shall help you if I can, but stay with us tonight and have no fear."

So they sat down again to supper and feasted merrily, and then all fell fast asleep, and Connor knew nothing more till he awoke in the morning and found himself in his own field.

"Now surely," thought he, "the adventure of last night was not all a dream, and I shall certainly find my cows when I go home; for that excellent, good young wolf promised his help, and I feel certain he would not deceive me."

But when he arrived home and looked over the yard and the stable and the field, there was no sign nor sight of the cows. So he grew very sad and dispirited. But just then he espied in the field close by three of the most beautiful strange cows he had ever set eyes on. "These must have strayed in," he said, "from some neighbor's ground"; and he took his big stick to drive them out of the gate off the field. But when he reached the gate, there stood a young black wolf watching; and when the cows tried to pass out at the gate he bit at them, and drove them back. Then Connor knew that his friend the wolf had kept his word. So he let the cows go quietly back to the field; and there they remained, and grew to be the finest in the whole country, and their descendants are flourishing to this day, and Connor grew rich and prospered; for a kind deed is never lost, but brings good luck to the doer forevermore, as the old proverb says:

> "Blessings are won,
> By a good deed done."

But never again did Connor find that desolate heath or that lone shieling, though he sought far and wide, to return his thanks, as was due to the friendly wolves; nor did he ever again meet any of the family, though he mourned much whenever a slaughtered wolf was brought into the town for the sake of the reward, fearing his excellent friend might be the victim.

The Phantom Horses

WHITSUNTIDE is a very fatal and unlucky time. Especially beware of water then, for there is an evil spirit in it, and no one should venture to bathe, nor to sail in a boat for fear of being drowned; nor to go a journey where water has to be crossed. And everything in the house must be sprinkled with holy water at Whitsuntide to keep away the fairies, who at that season are very active and malicious, and bewitch the cattle, and carry off the young children, and come up from the sea to hold strange midnight revels, when they kill with their fairy darts the unhappy mortal who crosses their path and pries at their mysteries.

There was a widow woman with one son, who had a nice farm of her own close to a lake, and she took great pains in the cultivation of the land, and her corn was the best in the whole country. But when nearly ripe, and just fit for cutting, she found to her dismay that every night it was trampled down and cruelly damaged; yet no one could tell by what means it was done.

So she set her son to watch. And at midnight he heard a great noise and a rushing of waves on the beach, and up out of the lake came a great troop of horses, who began to graze the corn and trample it down madly with their hoofs.

When he told all this to his mother she bade him watch the next night also, but to take several of the men with him furnished with bridles, and when the horses rose from the lake they were to fling the bridles over as many as they could catch.

Now at midnight there was the same noise heard again, and the rush of the waves, and in an instant all the field was filled with the fairy horses, grazing the corn and trampling it down. The men pursued them, but only succeeded in capturing one, and he was the noblest of the lot. The rest all plunged back into the lake. However, the men brought home the captured horse to the widow, and he was put in the stable and grew big and strong, and never another horse came up out of the lake, nor was the corn touched after that night of his capture. But when a year had passed by the widow said it was a shame to keep so fine a horse idle, and she bade the young man, her son, take him out to the hunt that was held that day by all the great gentry of the country, for it was Whitsuntide.

And, in truth, the horse carried him splendidly at the hunt, and everyone admired both the fine young rider and his steed. But as he was returning home, when they came within sight of the lake from which the fairy steed had risen, he began to plunge violently, and finally threw his rider. And the young man's foot being unfortunately caught in the stirrup, he was dragged along till he was torn limb from limb, while the horse still continued galloping on madly to the water, leaving some fragment of the unhappy lad after him on the road, till they reached the margin of the lake, when the horse shook off the last limb of the dead youth from him, and plunging into the waves disappeared from sight.

The people reverently gathered up the remains of the dead, and erected a monument of stones over the lad in a field by the edge of the lake; and everyone that passes by still lays a stone and says a prayer that the spirit of the dead may rest in peace.

The phantom horses were never seen again, but the lake has an evil reputation even to this day amongst the people; and no one would venture a boat on it after sundown at Whitsuntide, or during the time of the ripening of the corn, or when the harvest is ready for the sickle, for strange sounds are heard at night, like the wild galloping of a horse across the meadow, along with the cries as of a man in his death agony.

The Monstrous Cats

MANY strange things have happened on the island of Shark according to the narration of the islanders, who are extremely accurate in all the details they give, and never exaggerate, only tell the simple truth, which we are bound to accept unquestioned; for the people are too simple to invent. They only tell in their plain, unvarnished idiom what they have seen or heard.

They tell a story of a man on the island called Dermot, whose wife died of a fever, leaving two children, a boy and a girl. The girl died a year and a day after the mother, but the boy throve well, until one day when the fever seized him, and he cried out that his mother had come for him, and was calling him. And he asked for a drink of water, but there was none in the house. So a girl took a can and ran down to the well to fill it; and as she was stooping down a black shadow fell on her and covered her. Then she saw the dead mother close beside her, and nearly fainted with fright.

"Never fear, Mary *alanna*," said the woman, "but do as I bid you. When you go home, you will see a black cock by the head of the child's bed. This is the Spirit of Death come to carry away the boy; but you must prevent him. Therefore do as I tell you. Batch a crowing hen and kill her, and sprinkle the blood over the bed, and take ten straws and throw the tenth away, and stir the blood with the rest; then lay them on the child, and he will sleep and do well." On this the dead woman vanished, and the girl went home and did as she was ordered; the hen was killed, and the blood sprinkled. And the boy slept after the blood touched him, and slept on and on till the morning. Then he sat up and asked for food, and said he was now quite well, and must go and play. So they let him get up, and he was as strong as ever, and no harm came to him anymore.

And the heart of the father was glad that the child was given back to him through the sprinkling of the blood.

Now it happened that about three months after, a child of one of the neighbors grew sick, and was like to die. Then the man's wife rose up and said: "See, now, our child is like to die, but look how Dermot cured his son through the sprinkling of blood. Let us do the like."

So they caught a crowing hen and killed her, and sprinkled the blood over the sick child. But, lo! a terrible thing happened, for the door was flung open, and in walked two monstrous black cats.

"How dare you kill my kitten?" said one of them. "My darling, only kitten! But you shall suffer for it."

"Ay," said the other, "we'll teach you how to insult a royal cat again, and kill one of our great race just to save your own wretched child," and they flew at the man and tore his face and hands. Then the wife rushed at them with the churn-dash, while the man strove to defend himself with a spade. But all the same the cats had the best of it, and clawed and tore and scratched till the miserable pair could not see for the blood streaming down their faces.

Luckily, however, the neighbors, hearing the scrimmage, rushed in and helped to fight the cats; but soon they had to fly, for the cats were too strong for them, and not a soul could stand before them. However, at last the cats grew tired, and after licking their paws and washing their faces, they moved towards the door to go away, first saying to the man: "Now we have done enough to punish you for this time, and your baby will live, for Death can take but one this night, and he has taken our child. So yours is safe, and this we swear by the blood, and by the power of the great king of the cats."

So they whisked out of the house, and were never more seen by man or mortal on the island of Shark.

6.
LEPRECHAUNS
AND A
PHOUKA

The Leprechaun

THE Leprechauns are merry, industrious, tricksy little sprites, who do all the shoemaker's work and the tailor's and the cobbler's for the fairy gentry, and are often seen at sunset under the hedge singing and stitching. They know all the secrets of hidden treasure, and if they take a fancy to a person will guide him to the spot in the fairy rath where the pot of gold lies buried. It is believed that a family now living near Castlerea came by their riches in a strange way, all through the good offices of a friendly Leprechaun. And the legend has been handed down through many generations as an established fact.

There was a poor boy once who used to drive his cart of turf daily back and forward, and make what money he could by the sale; but he was a strange boy, very silent and moody, and the people said he was a fairy changeling, for he joined in no sports and scarcely ever spoke to anyone, but spent the nights reading all the old bits of books he picked up in his rambles. The one thing he longed for above all was to get rich, and to be able to give up the old weary turf cart, and live in peace and quietness, with nothing but books round him, in a beautiful house and garden all by himself.

Now he had read in the old books how the Leprechauns knew all the secret places where gold lay hid, and day by day he watched for a sight of the little cobbler, and listened for the click, click of his hammer as he sat under the hedge mending the shoes.

At last, one evening just as the sun set, he saw a little fellow under a dock leaf, working away, dressed all in green, with a cocked hat on his head. So the boy jumped down from the cart and seized him by the neck.

"Now, you don't stir from this," he cried, "till you tell me where to find the hidden gold."

"Easy now," said the Leprechaun, "don't hurt me, and I will tell you all about it. But mind you, I could hurt you if I chose, for I have the power; but I won't do it, for we are cousins once removed. So as we are near relations I'll just be good, and show you the place of the secret gold that none can have or keep except those of fairy blood and race. Come along with me, then, to the old fort of Lipenshaw, for there it lies. But make haste, for when the last red glow of the sun vanishes the gold will disappear also, and you will never find it again."

"Come off, then," said the boy, and he carried the Leprechaun into the turf cart, and drove off. And in a second they were at the old fort, and went in through a door made in the stone wall.

"Now, look round," said the Leprechaun; and the boy saw the whole ground covered with gold pieces, and there were vessels of silver lying about in such plenty that all the riches of all the world seemed gathered there.

"Now take what you want," said the Leprechaun, "but hasten, for if that door shuts you will never leave this place as long as you live."

So the boy gathered up his arms full of gold and silver, and flung them into the cart; and was on his way back for more when the door shut with a clap like thunder, and all the place became dark as night. And he saw no more of the Leprechaun, and had not time even to thank him.

So he thought it best to drive home at once with his treasure, and when he arrived and was alone he counted his riches and all the bright yellow gold pieces, enough for a king's ransom.

And he was very wise and told no one; but went off next day to Dublin and put all his treasures into the bank, and found that he was now indeed as rich as a lord.

So he ordered a fine house to be built with spacious gardens, and he had servants and carriages and books to his heart's content. And he gathered all the wise men round him to give him the learning of a gentleman; and he became a great and powerful man in the country, where his memory is still held in high honor, and his descendants are living to this day rich and prosperous; for their wealth has never decreased though they have ever given largely to the poor, and are noted above all things for the friendly heart and the liberal hand.

LEPRECHAUNS AND A PHOUKA

The Hidden Gold

Leprechauns can be bitterly malicious if they are offended, and one should be very cautious in dealing with them, and always treat them with great civility, or they will take revenge and never reveal the secret of the hidden gold.

One day a young lad was out in the fields at work when he saw a little fellow, not the height of his hand, mending shoes under a dock leaf. And he went over, never taking his eyes off him for fear he would vanish away; and when he got quite close he made a grab at the creature, and lifted him up and put him in his pocket.

Then he ran away home as fast as he could, and when he had the Leprechaun safe in the house, he tied him by an iron chain to the hob.

"Now, tell me," he said, "where am I to find a pot of gold? Let me know the place or I'll punish you."

"I know of no pot of gold," said the Leprechaun; "but let me go that I may finish mending the shoes."

"Then I'll make you tell me," said the lad.

And with that he made down a great fire, and put the little fellow on it and scorched him.

"Oh, take me off, take me off!" cried the Leprechaun, "and I'll tell you. Just there, under the dock leaf, where you found me, there is a pot of gold. Go; dig and find."

So the lad was delighted, and ran to the door; but it so happened that his mother was just then coming in with the pail of fresh milk, and in his haste he knocked the pail out of her hand, and all the milk was spilled on the floor.

Then, when the mother saw the Leprechaun, she grew very angry and beat him. "Go away, you little wretch!" she cried. "You have overlooked the milk and brought ill-luck." And she kicked him out of the house.

But the lad ran off to find the dock leaf, though he came back very sorrowful in the evening, for he had dug and dug nearly down to the middle of the earth; but no pot of gold was to be seen.

That same night the husband was coming home from his work, and as he passed the old fort he heard voices and laughter, and one said, "They are looking for a pot of gold; but they little know that a crock of gold is lying down in the bottom of the old quarry, hid under the stones close by the garden wall. But whoever gets it must go of a dark night at twelve o'clock, and beware of bring-ing his wife with him."

So the man hurried home and told his wife he would go that very night, for it was black dark, and she must stay at home and watch for him, and not stir from the house till he came back. Then he went out into the dark night alone.

"Now," thought the wife, when he was gone, "if I could only get to the quarry before him I would have the pot of gold all to myself; while if he gets it I shall have nothing."

And with that she went out and ran like the wind until she reached the quarry, and than she she began to creep down very quietly in the black dark. But a great stone was in her path, and she stumbled over it, and fell down and down till she reached the bottom, and there she lay groaning, for her leg was broken by the fall.

Just then her husband came to the edge of the quarry and began to descend. But when he heard the groans he was frightened.

"Cross of Christ about us!" he exclaimed; "what is that down below? Is it evil, or is it good?"

"Oh, come down, come down and help me!" cried the woman. "It's your wife is here, and my leg is broken, and I'll die if you don't help me."

"And is this my pot of gold?" exclaimed the poor man. "Only my wife with a broken leg lying at the bottom of the quarry."

And he was at his wits' end to know what to do, for the night was so dark he could not see a hand before him. So he roused up a neighbor, and between them they dragged up the poor woman and carried her home, and laid her on the bed half dead from fright, and it was many a day before she was able to get about as usual; indeed she limped all her life long, so that the people said the curse of the Leprechaun was on her.

But as to the pot of gold, from that day to this not one of the family, father or son, or any belonging to them, ever set eyes on it. However, the little Leprechaun still sits under the dock leaf of the hedge and laughs at them as he mends the shoes with his little hammer—tick tack, tick tack—but they are afraid to touch him, for now they know he can take his revenge.

The Phouka

THE Phouka is a friendly being who often helps the farmer at his work if he is treated well and kindly.

One day a farmer's son was minding cattle in the field when something rushed past him like the wind; but he was not frightened, for he knew it was the Phouka on his way to the old mill by the moat where the fairies met every night. So he called out, "Phouka, Phouka! show me what you are like, and I'll give you my big coat to keep you warm." Then a young bull came to him lashing his tail like mad; but Phadrig threw the coat over him, and in a moment he was quiet as a lamb, and told the boy to come to the mill that night when the moon was up, and he would have good luck.

So Phadrig went, but saw nothing except sacks of corn all lying about on the ground, for the men had fallen asleep, and no work was done. Then he lay down also and slept, for he was very tired; and when he woke up early in the morning there was all the meal ground, though certainly the men had not done it, for they still slept. And this happened for three nights, after which Phadrig determined to keep awake and watch.

Now there was an old chest in the mill, and he crept into this to hide, and just looked through the keyhole to see what would happen. And exactly at midnight six little fellows came in, each

carrying a sack of corn upon his back; and after them came an old man in tattered rags of clothes, and he bade them turn the mill, and they turned and turned till all was ground.

Then Phadrig ran to tell his father, and the miller determined to watch the next night with his son, and both together saw the same thing happen.

"Now," said the farmer, "I see it is the Phouka's work, and let him work if it pleases him, for the men are idle and lazy and only sleep. So I'll pack the whole set off tomorrow, and leave the grinding of the corn to this excellent old Phouka."

After this the farmer grew so rich that there was no end to his money, for he had no men to pay, and all his corn was ground without his spending a penny. Of course the people wondered much over his riches, but he never told them about the Phouka, or their curiosity would have spoiled the luck.

Now Phadrig went often to the mill and hid in the chest that he might watch the fairies at work; but he had great pity for the poor old Phouka in his tattered clothes, who yet directed everything and had hard work of it sometimes keeping the little Phoukas in order. So Phadrig, out of love and gratitude, bought a fine suit of cloth and silk and laid it one night on the floor of the mill just where the old Phouka always stood to give his orders to the little men, and then he crept into the chest to watch.

"How is this?" said the Phouka when he saw the clothes. "Are these for me? I shall be turned into a fine gentleman."

And he put them on, and then began to walk up and down admiring himself. But suddenly he remembered the corn and went to grind as usual, then stopped and cried out, "No, no. No more work for me. Fine gentlemen don't grind corn. I'll go out and see a little of the world and show my fine clothes." And he kicked away the old rags into a corner, and went out.

No corn was ground that night, nor the next, nor the next; all the little Phoukas ran away, and not a sound was heard in the mill. Then Phadrig grew very sorry for the loss of his old friend, and used to go out into the fields and call out, "Phouka, Phouka! come back to me. Let me see your face." But the old Phouka never came back, and all his life long Phadrig never looked on the face of his friend again. However, the farmer had made so much money that he wanted no more help; and he sold the mill, and reared up Phadrig to be a great scholar and a gentleman, who had his own house and land and servants. And in time he married a beautiful lady, so beautiful that the people said she must be daughter to the king of the fairies.

A strange thing happened at the wedding, for when they all stood up to drink the bride's health, Phadrig saw beside him a golden cup filled with wine. And no one knew how the golden cup had come to his hand; but Phadrig guessed it was the Phouka's gift, and he drank the wine without fear and made his bride drink also. And ever after their lives were happy and prosperous, and the golden cup was kept as a treasure in the family, and the descendants of Phadrig have it in their possession to this day.

7.
MAGIC
SPELLS

The Butter Mystery

THERE were two brothers who had a small farm and dairy between them, and they were honest and industrious, and worked hard to get along, though they had barely enough, after all their labor, just to keep body and soul together.

One day while churning, the handle of the dash broke, and nothing being near to mend it, one of the brothers cut off a branch from an elder tree that grew close to the house, and tied it to the dash for a handle. Then the churning went on, but to their surprise, the butter gathered so thick that all the crocks in the house were soon full, and still there was more left. The same thing went on every churning day, so the brothers became rich, for they could fill the market with their butter, and still had more than enough for every buyer.

At last, being honest and true men, they began to fear that there was witchcraft in it, and that they were wronging their neighbors by abstracting their butter, and bringing it to their own churn in some strange way. So they both went off together to a great fairy doctor, and told him the whole story, and asked his advice.

"Foolish men," he said to them, "why did you come to me? for now you have broken the spell, and you will never have your crocks filled with butter anymore. Your good fortune has passed away, for know the truth now. You were not wronging your neighbors; all was fair and just that you did, but this is how it happened. Long ago, the fairies passing through your land had a dispute and fought a battle, and having no arms, they flung lumps of butter at each other, which got lodged in the branches of the elder tree in great quantities, for it was just after May Eve, when butter is plenty. This is the butter you have had, for the elder tree has a sacred power which preserved it until now, and it came down to you through the branch you cut for a handle to the dash. But the spell is broken now that you have uttered the mystery, and you will have no more butter from the elder tree."

Then the brothers went away sorrowful, and never after did the butter come beyond the usual quantity. However, they had already made so much money that they were content. And they stocked their farm, and all things prospered with them, for they had dealt uprightly in the matter, and the blessing of the Lord was on them.

The Wicked Widow

Evil spells over milk and butter are generally practiced by women, and arise from some feeling of malice or envy against a prosperous neighbor. But the spell will not work unless some portion of the milk is first given by consent. The people therefore are very reluctant to give away milk, unless to some friend that they could not suspect of evil. Tramps coming in to beg for a mug of milk should always be avoided; they may be witches in disguise; and even if milk is given, it must be drunk in the house, and not carried away out of it. In every case the person who enters must give a hand to the churn, and say, "God bless all here."

A young farmer, one of the fine handsome fellows of the West, named Hugh Connor, who was also well off and rich, took to wife a pretty young girl of the village called Mary, one of the Leydons, and there was no better girl in all the country round, and they were very comfortable and happy together. But Hugh Connor had been keeping company before his marriage with a young widow of the place, who had designs on him, and was filled with rage when Mary Leydon was selected for Connor's bride, in place of herself. Then a desire for vengeance rose up in her heart, and she laid her plans accordingly.

First, she got a fairy woman to teach her some witch secrets and spells, and then by great pretence of love and affection for Mary Connor, she got frequent admission to the house, soothing and flattering the young wife; and on churning days she would especially make it a point to come in and offer a helping hand, and if the cakes were on the griddle, she would sit down to watch and turn them. But it so happened that always on these days the cakes were sure to be burned and spoiled, and the butter would not rise in the churn, or if any did come, it was sour and bad, and of no use for the market. But still the widow kept on visiting, and soothing, and flattering, till Mary Connor thought she was the very best friend to her in the whole wide world, though it was true that whenever the widow came to the house something evil happened. The best dish fell down of itself off the dresser and broke; or the rain got in through the roof, and Mary's new cashmere gown, a present that had come to her all the way from Dublin, was quite ruined and spoiled. But worse came, for the cow sickened, and a fine young brood of turkeys walked straight into the lake and got drowned. And still worst of all, the picture of the Blessed Virgin Mother that was pinned up to the wall, fell down one day, and was blown into the fire and burned.

After this, what luck could be on the house? And Mary's heart sank within her, and she fairly broke down, and cried her very life out in a torrent of tears.

Now it so happened that an old woman with a blue cloak, and the hood of it over her head, a stranger, was passing by at the time, and she stepped in and asked Mary kindly what ailed her. So Mary told her all her misfortunes, and how everything in the house seemed bewitched for evil.

"Now," said the stranger, "I see it all, for I am wise, and know the mysteries. Some one with the Evil Eye comes to your house. We must find out who it is."

Then Mary told her that the nearest friend she had was the widow, but she was so sweet and kind, no one could suspect her of harm.

"We'll see," said the stranger. "Only do as I bid you, and have everything ready when she comes."

"She will be here soon," said Mary, "for it is churning day, and she always comes to help exactly at noon."

"Then I'll begin at once; and now close the door fast," said the stranger.

And with that she threw some herbs on the fire, so that a great smoke arose. Then she took all the plough irons that were about, and one of them she drove into the ground close beside the churn, and put a live coal beside it; and the other irons she heated red-hot in the fire, and still threw on more herbs to make a thick smoke, which Mary thought smelt like the incense in the church. Then with a hot iron rod from the fire, the strange woman made the sign of the cross on the threshold, and another over the hearth. After which a loud roaring was heard outside, and the widow rushed in crying out that a hot stick was running through her heart, and all her body was on fire. And then she dropped down on the floor in a fit, and her face became quite black, and her limbs worked in convulsions.

"Now," said the stranger, "you see who it is put the Evil Eye on all your house; but the spell has been broken at last. Send for the men to carry her back to her own house, and never let that witch-woman cross your threshold again."

After this the stranger disappeared, and was seen no more in the village.

Now when all the neighbors heard the story, they would have no dealings with the widow. She was shunned and hated; and no respectable person would be seen talking to her, and she went by the name of the Evil Witch. So her life was very miserable, and not long after she died of sheer vexation and spite, all by herself alone, for no one would go near her; and the night of the wake no one went to offer a prayer, for they said the devil would be there in person to look after his own. And no one would walk with her coffin to the grave, for they said the devil was waiting at the churchyard gate for her; and they firmly believe to this day that her body was carried away on that night from the graveyard by the powers of darkness. But no one ventured to test the truth of the story by opening the coffin, so the weird legend remains still unsolved.

But as for Hugh Connor and the pretty Mary, they prospered after that in all things, and good luck and the blessing of God seemed to be evermore on them and their house, and their cattle, and their children. At the same time, Mary never omitted on churning days to put a red-hot horseshoe under the churn according as told her by the stranger, who she firmly believed was a good fairy in disguise, who came to help her in the time of her sore trouble and anxiety.

A Spell of Apples

It is said by the wise women and fairy doctors that the roots of the elder tree, and the roots of an apple tree that bears red apples, if boiled together and drunk fasting, will expel any evil living thing or evil spirit that may have taken up its abode in the body of a man.

But an evil charm to produce a living thing in the body can also be made, by pronouncing a certain magic and wicked spell over the food or drink taken by any person that an enemy wishes to injure.

One should therefore be very cautious in accepting anything to eat from a person of known malicious tongue and spiteful heart, or who has an ill will against you, for poison lies in their glance and in the touch of their hands; and an evil spell is in their very presence, and on all they do, say, or touch.

Cathal, king of Munster, was the tallest and handsomest of all the kings of Erin, and he fell deeply in love with the beautiful sister of Fergus, king of Ulster; and the lovers were happy in their love and resolved on marriage. But Fergus, King of the North, had a mortal hatred to Cathal, King of the South, and wished, in secret, to prevent the marriage. So he set a watch over his sister, and by this means found out that she was sending a basket of the choicest apples to her lover, by the hands of a trusty messenger. On this Fergus managed to get hold of the basket of fruit from the messenger; and he changed them secretly for another lot of apples, over which he worked an evil spell. Furnished with these the messenger set out for Cashel, and presented them to Cathal the king, who, delighted at this proof of love from his princess, began at once to eat the apples. But the more he ate, the more he longed for them, for a wicked spell was on every apple. When he had eaten them all up, he sent round the country for more, and ate, and ate, until there was not an apple left in Cashel, nor in all the country round.

Then he bade his chieftains go forth and bring in food to appease his appetite; and he ate up all the cattle and the grain

and the fruit, and still cried for more; and had the houses searched for food to bring to him. So the people were in despair, for they had no more food, and starvation was over the land.

Now a great and wise man, the chief poet of his tribe, happened to be travelling through Munster at that time, and hearing of the king's state, he greatly desired to see him, for he knew there was devil's work in the evil spell. So they brought him to the king, and many strong invocations he uttered over him, and many powerful incantations, for poets have a knowledge of mysteries above all other men; until finally, after three days had passed, he announced to the lords and chiefs that on that night, when the moon rose, the spell would be broken, and the king restored to his wonted health. So all the chiefs gathered round in the courtyard to watch; but no one was allowed to enter the room where the king lay, save only the poet. And he was to give the signal when the hour had come and the spell was broken.

So as they watched, and just as the moon rose, a great cry was heard from the king's room, and the poet, flinging open the door, bade the chiefs enter; and there on the floor lay a huge dead wolf, who for a whole year had taken up his abode in the king's body; but was now happily cast forth by the strong incantations of the poet.

After this the king fell into a deep sleep, and when he arose he was quite well, and strong again as ever, in all the pride of his youth and beauty. At this the people rejoiced much, for he was greatly loved, and the poet who had restored him was honored above all men in the land; for the king himself took off the golden torque from his own neck, and placed it on that of the poet, and he set him at his right hand at the feast.

Now a strange thing happened just at this time; for Fergus, King of the North, fell ill, and wasted away to a shadow, and of all the beautiful meats and wines they set before him he could taste nothing. So he died before a year had passed by; and then Cathal the king wedded his beloved princess, and they lived happily through many years.

The Evil Eye

THERE is nothing more dreaded by the people, nor considered more deadly in its effects, than the Evil Eye.

It may strike at any moment unless the greatest precautions are taken, and even then there is no true help possible unless the fairy doctor is at once summoned to pronounce the mystic charm that can alone destroy the evil and fatal influence.

There are several modes in which the Evil Eye can act, some much more deadly than others. If certain persons are met the first thing in the morning, you will be unlucky for the whole of that day in all you do. If the evil-eyed comes in to rest, and looks fixedly on anything, on cattle or on a child, there is doom in the glance—a fatality that cannot be evaded except by a powerful counter-charm. But if the evil-eyed mutters a verse over a sleeping child, that child will assuredly die, for the incantation is of the devil, and no charm has power to resist it or turn away the evil. Sometimes the process of bewitching is effected by looking fixedly at the object, through nine fingers; especially is the magic fatal if the victim is seated by the fire in the evening when the moon is full. Therefore, to avoid being suspected of having the Evil Eye, it is necessary at once, when looking at a child, to say "God bless it." And when passing a farmyard where the cows are collected for milking, to say, "The blessing of God be on you and on all your labors." If this form is omitted, the worst results may be apprehended, and the people would be filled with terror and alarm, unless a counter-charm were not instantly employed.

The singular malefic influence of a glance has been felt by most persons in life; an influence that seems to paralyze intellect and speech, simply by the mere presence in the room of someone who is mystically antipathetic to our nature. For the soul is like a fine-toned harp that vibrates to the slightest external force or movement, and the presence and glance of some persons can radiate around us a divine joy, while others may kill the soul with a sneer or a frown. We call these subtle influences mysteries, but the early races believed them to be produced by spirits, good or evil, as they acted on the nerves or the intellect.

A woman in the County Galway had a beautiful child, so handsome that all the neighbors were very careful to say "God bless it" when they saw him, for they knew the fairies would desire to steal the child, and carry it off to the hills.

But one day it chanced that an old woman, a stranger, came in. "Let me rest," she said, "for I am weary." And she sat down and looked at the child, but never said "God bless it." And when she had rested, she rose up, looked again at the child fixedly in silence, and then went her way.

All that night the child cried and would not sleep. And all next day it moaned as if in pain. So the mother told the priest, but he would do nothing for fear of the fairies. And just as the poor mother was in despair, she saw a strange woman going by the door. "Who knows," she said to her husband, "but this woman would help us." So they asked her to come in and rest. And when she looked at the child she said "God bless it," instantly, and spat three times at it, and then sat down.

"Now, what will you give me," she said, "if I tell you what ails the child?"

"I will cross your hand with silver," said the mother, "as much as you want, only speak," and she laid the money on the woman's hand. "Now tell me the truth, for the sake and in the name of Mary, and the good angels."

"Well," said the stranger, "the fairies have had your child these two days in the hills, and this is a changeling they have left in its place. But so many blessings were said on your child that the fairies can do it no harm. For there was only one blessing wanting, and only one person gave the Evil Eye. Now, you must watch for this woman, carry her into the house and secretly cut off a piece of her cloak. Then burn the piece close to the child, till the smoke as it rises makes him sneeze; and when this happens the spell is broken, and your own child will come back to you safe and sound, in place of the changeling."

Then the stranger rose up and went her way.

All that evening the mother watched for the old woman, and at last she spied her on the road.

"Come in," she cried, "come in, good woman, and rest, for the cakes are hot on the griddle, and supper is ready."

So the woman came in, but never said, "God bless you kindly," to man or mortal, only scowled at the child, who cried worse than ever.

Now the mother had told her eldest girl to cut off a piece of the old woman's cloak, secretly, when she sat down to eat. And the girl did what was desired, and handed the piece to her mother, unknown to anyone. But, to their surprise, this was no sooner done than the woman rose up and went out without uttering a word, and they saw her no more.

Then the father carried the child outside, and burned the piece of cloth before the door, and held the boy over the smoke till he sneezed three times violently, after which he gave the child back to the mother, who laid him in his bed, where he slept peacefully, with a smile on his face, and cried no more with the cry of pain. And when he woke up the mother knew that she had got her own darling child back from the fairies, and no evil thing happened to him anymore.

The Legend of Ballytowtas Castle

In old times there lived where Ballytowtas Castle now stands a poor man named Towtas. It was in the time when manna fell to the earth with the dew of evening, and Towtas lived by gathering the manna, and thus supported himself, for he was a poor man, and had nothing else.

One day a pedlar came by that way with a fair young daughter.

"Give us a night's lodging," he said to Towtas, "for we are weary."

And Towtas did so.

Next morning, when they were going away, his heart longed for the young girl, and he said to the pedlar, "Give me your daughter for my wife."

"How will you support her?" asked the pedlar.

"Better than you can," answered Towtas, "for she can never want."

Then he told him all about the manna; how he went out every morning when it was lying on the ground with the dew, and gathered it, as his father and forefathers had done before him, and lived on it all their lives, so that he had never known want nor any of his people.

Then the girl showed she would like to stay with the young man, and the pedlar consented, and they were married, Towtas and the fair young maiden; and the pedlar left them and went his way. So years went on, and they were very happy and never wanted; and they had one son, Towtas, a bright, handsome youth, as clever as he was comely.

But in due time old Towtas died, and after her husband was buried, the woman went out to gather the manna as she had seen him do, when the dew lay on the ground; but she soon grew tired and said to herself, "Why should I do this thing every day? I'll just gather enough now to do the week and then I can rest."

So she gathered up great heaps of it greedily, and went into the house. But the sin of greediness lay on her evermore; and not a bit of manna fell with the dew that evening, nor ever again. And she was poor, and faint with hunger, and had to go out and work in the fields to earn the morsel that kept her and her son alive; and she begged pence from the people as they went into chapel, and this paid for her son's schooling; so he went on with his learning, and no one in the county was like him for beauty and knowledge.

One day he heard the people talking of a great lord that lived up in Dublin, who had a daughter so handsome that her like was never seen; and all the fine young gentlemen were dying about her, but she would take none of them. And he came home to his mother and said, "I shall go see this great lord's daughter. Maybe the luck will be mine above all the fine young gentlemen that love her."

"Go along, poor fool," said the mother, "how can the poor stand before the rich?"

But he persisted. "If I die on the road," he said, "I'll try it."

"Wait, then," she answered, "till Sunday, and whatever I get I'll give you half of it." So she gave him half of the pence she gathered at the chapel door, and bid him go in the name of God.

He hadn't gone far when he met a poor man who asked him for a trifle for God's sake. So he gave him something out of his mother's money and went on. Again, another met him, and begged for a trifle to buy food, for the sake of God, and he gave him something also, and then went on.

"Give me a trifle for God's sake," cried a voice, and he saw a third poor man before him.

"I have nothing left," said Towtas, "but a few pence; if I give them, I shall have nothing for food and must die of hunger. But come with me, and whatever I can buy for this I shall share with you." And as they were going on to the inn, he told his story to the beggar man—how he wanted to go to Dublin, but had now no money. So they came to the inn, and he called for a loaf and a drink of milk. "Cut the loaf," he said to the beggar. "You are the oldest."

"I won't," said the other, but Towtas made him.

And so the beggar cut the loaf, but though they ate, it never grew smaller, and though they drank as they liked of the milk, it never grew less. Then Towtas rose up to pay, but when the landlady came and looked, "How is this?" she said. "You have eaten nothing. I'll not take your money, poor boy," but he made her take some; and they left the place, and went on their way together.

"Now," said the beggar man, "you have been three times good to me today, for thrice I have met you, and you gave me help for the sake of God each time. See, now, I can help also," and he reached a gold ring to the handsome youth. "Wherever you place that ring, and wish for it, gold will come—bright gold, so that you can never want while you have it."

Then Towtas put the ring first in one pocket and then in another, until all his pockets were so heavy with gold that he could scarcely walk; but when he turned to thank the friendly beggar man, he had disappeared.

So, wondering to himself at all his adventures, he went on, until he came at last in sight of the lord's palace, which was beautiful to see; but he would not enter in until he went and bought fine clothes, and made himself as grand as any prince; and then he went boldly up, and they invited him in, for they said, "Surely he is a king's son." And when dinner-hour came the lord's daughter linked her arm with Towtas, and smiled on him. And he drank of the rich wine, and was mad with love; but at last the wine overcame him, and the servants had to carry him to his bed; and in going into his room he dropped the ring from his finger, but knew it not.

Now, in the morning, the lord's daughter came by, and cast her eyes upon the door of his chamber, and there close by it was the ring she had seen him wear.

"Ah," she said, "I'll tease him now about his ring." And she put it in her box, and wished that she were as rich as a king's daughter, that so the king's son might marry her; and, behold, the box filled up with gold, so that she could not shut it; and she put it from her into another box, and that filled also; and then she was frightened at the ring, and put it at last in her pocket as the safest place.

But when Towtas awoke and missed the ring, his heart was grieved.

"Now, indeed," he said, "my luck is gone."

And he inquired of all the servants, and then of the lord's daughter, and she laughed, by which he knew she had it; but no coaxing would get it from her, so when all was useless he went away, and set out again to reach his old home.

And he was very mournful and threw himself down on the ferns near an old fort, waiting till night came on, for he feared to go home in the daylight lest the people should laugh at him for his folly. And about dusk three cats came out of the fort talking to each other.

"How long our cook is away," said one.

"What can have happened to him?" said another.

And as they were grumbling a fourth cat came up.

"What delayed you?" they all asked angrily.

Then he told his story—how he had met Towtas and given him the ring. "And I just went," he said, "to the lord's palace to see how the young man behaved; and I was leaping over the dinner table when the lord's knife struck my tail and three drops of blood fell upon his plate, but he never saw it and swallowed them with his meat. So now he has three kittens inside him and is dying of agony, and can never be cured until he drinks three draughts of the water of the well of Ballytowtas."

So when young Towtas heard the cats talk he sprang up and went and told his mother to give him three bottles full of the water of the Towtas well, and he would go to the lord disguised as a doctor and cure him.

So off he went to Dublin. And all the doctors in Ireland were round the lord, but none of them could tell what ailed him, or how to cure him. Then Towtas came in and said, "I will cure him." So they gave him entertainment and lodging, and when he was refreshed he gave of the well water three draughts to his lordship, when out jumped the three kittens. And there was great rejoicing, and they treated Towtas like a prince. But all the same he could not get the ring from the lord's daughter, so he set off home again quite disheartened, and thought to himself, "If I could only meet the man again that gave me the ring, who knows

what luck I might have?" And he sat down to rest in a wood, and saw there not far off three boys fighting under an oak tree.

"Shame on ye to fight so," he said to them. "What is the fight about?"

Then they told him. "Our father," they said, "before he died, buried under this oak tree a ring by which you can be in any place in two minutes if you only wish it; a goblet that is always full when standing, and empty only when on its side; and a harp that plays any tune of itself that you name or wish for."

"I want to divide the things," said the youngest boy, "and let us all go and seek our fortunes as we can."

"But I have a right to the whole," said the eldest.

They went on fighting, till at length Towtas said, "I'll tell you how to settle the matter. All of you be here tomorrow. I'll think over the matter tonight, and I engage you will have nothing more to quarrel about when you come in the morning."

So the boys promised to keep good friends till they met in the morning, and went away.

When Towtas saw them clear off, he dug up the ring, the goblet, and the harp, and now said he, "I'm all right, and they won't have anything to fight about in the morning."

Off he set back again to the lord's castle with the ring, the goblet, and the harp; but he soon bethought himself of the powers of the ring, and in two minutes he was in the great hall where all the lords and ladies were just sitting down to dinner; and the harp played the sweetest music, and they all listened in delight; and he drank out of the goblet which was never empty, and then, when his head began to grow a little light, "It is enough," he said; and putting his arm round the waist of the lord's daughter, he took his harp and goblet in the other hand, and murmuring, "I wish we were at the old fort by the side of the wood," in two minutes they were both at the desired spot. But his head was heavy with the wine, and he laid down the harp beside him and fell asleep. And when she saw him asleep she took the ring off his finger, and the harp and the goblet from the ground and was home in her father's castle before two minutes had passed by.

When Towtas awoke and found his prize gone, and all his treasures besides, he was like one mad; and roamed about the country till he came by an orchard, where he saw a tree covered with bright, rosy apples. Being hungry and thirsty, he plucked one and ate it, but no sooner had he done so than horns began to sprout from his forehead, and grew larger and longer till he knew he looked like a goat, and all he could do, they would not come off. Now, indeed, he was driven out of his mind, and thought how all the neighbors would laugh at him; and as he raged and roared with shame, he spied another tree with apples, still brighter, of ruddy gold.

"If I were to have fifty pairs of horns I must have one of those," he said; and seizing one, he had no sooner tasted it than the horns fell off, and he felt that he was looking stronger and handsomer than ever.

"Now, I have her at last," he exclaimed. "I'll put horns on them all, and will never take them off until they give her to me as my bride before the whole Court."

Without further delay he set off to the lord's palace, carrying with him as many of the apples as he could bring off the two trees. And when they saw the beauty of the fruit they longed for it; and he gave to them all, so that at last there was not a head to be seen without horns in the whole dining hall. Then they cried out and prayed to have the horns taken off, but Towtas said, "No; there they shall be till I have the lord's daughter given to me for my bride, and my two rings, my goblet, and my harp all restored to me."

And this was done before the face of all the lords and ladies; and his treasures were restored to him; and the lord placed his daughter's hand in the hand of Towtas, saying, "Take her; she is your wife. Only free me from the horns."

Then Towtas brought forth the golden apples; and they all ate, and the horns fell off; and he took his bride and his treasures, and carried them off home, where he built the Castle of Bally-towtas, in the place where stood his father's hut, and enclosed the well within the walls. And when he had filled his treasure-room with gold, so that no man could count his riches, he buried his fairy treasures deep in the ground, where no man knew, and no man has ever yet been able to find them until this day.

The Fenian Knights

WHEN the great Fionn Ma-Coul was quite a youth, he was taken prisoner by a one-eyed giant, who at first was going to kill him, but then changed his mind and sent him to the kitchen to mind the dinner. Now there was a great and splendid salmon broiling on the fire, and the giant said, "Watch that salmon till it is done; but if a single blister rise on the skin, you shall be killed."

Then the giant threw himself down to sleep while waiting for the dinner.

So Fionn watched the salmon with all his eyes, but to his horror saw a blister rising on the beautiful silver skin of the fish, and in his fright and eagerness, he pressed his thumb down on it to flatten it; then the pain of the burn being great, he clapped the thumb into his mouth and kept it there to suck out the fire. When he drew it back, however, he found, to his surprise, that he had a knowledge of all that was going to happen to him, and a clear sense of what he ought to do. And it came into his mind that if he put out the giant's eye with an iron rod heated in the fire, he could escape from the monster. So he heated the rod, and while the giant slept, he plunged it into his eye, and before the horrid being recovered from the shock, Fionn escaped and was soon back safe amongst his own people, the Fenian knights; and ever after in moments of great peril and doubt, when he put his thumb into his mouth and sucked it, the vision of the future came on him and he could foresee clearly whatever danger lay in his path and how to avoid it. But it was only in such extreme moments of peril that the mystic power was granted to him. And thus he was enabled to save his own life and the lives of his chosen Fenian guard when all hope seemed well-nigh gone, as you will see in the following story.

There is a fort near the Killeries in Connemara called *Lis-na-Keeran*. One day the powerful chief that lived there invited Fionn Ma-Coul, with his son Oscar and a band of Fenian knights, to a great banquet. But when the guests arrived they found no chairs prepared for them, only rough benches of wood placed round the table.

So Oscar and his father would take no place, but stood watching, for they suspected treachery. The knights, however, fearing nothing, sat down to the feast, but were instantly fixed to the benches so firmly by magic that they could neither rise nor move.

Then Fionn began to chew his thumb, from which he always derived knowledge of the future, and by his magic power he saw clearly a great and terrible warrior riding fiercely towards the fort, and Fionn knew that unless he could be stopped before crossing a certain ford, they must all die, for they had been brought to Lis-na-Keeran only to be slain by their treacherous host; and unless the warrior was killed and his blood sprinkled on the Fenian knights, they must remain fixed on the wooden benches forever.

So Oscar of the Lion Heart rushed forth to the encounter. And he flung his spear at the mighty horseman, and they fought desperately till the setting of the sun. Then at last Oscar triumphed; victory was his; and he cut off the head of his adversary, and carried it on his spear all bleeding to the fort, where he let the blood drop down upon the Fenian knights that were transfixed by magic. On this they at once sprang up free and scatheless, all except one, for on him unhappily no blood had fallen, and so he remained fixed to the bench. His companions tried to drag him up by main force, but as they did so the skin of his thighs was left on the bench, and he was like to die.

Then they killed a sheep, and wrapped the fleece round him warm from the animal to heal him. So he was cured, but ever after, strange to relate, seven stone of wool were annually shorn from his body as long as he lived.

8.
THE POWER
OF POETS

The Poet and the Farmer's Daughter

It was believed that the power of fascination by the glance, which is not necessarily an evil power like the Evil Eye, was possessed in a remarkable degree by learned and wise people, especially poets, so that they could make themselves loved and followed by any girl they liked, simply by the influence of the glance.

About the year 1790, a young man resided in the County Limerick who had this power of the glance in a singular and unusual degree. He was a clever, witty rhymer in the Irish language; and, probably, had the deep poet eyes that characterize warm and passionate poet-natures—eyes that even without necromancy have been known to exercise a powerful magnetic influence over female minds.

One day, while travelling far from home, he came upon a bright, pleasant-looking farmhouse, and feeling weary, he stopped and requested a drink of milk and leave to rest. The farmer's daughter, a young, handsome girl, not liking to admit a stranger, as all the maids were churning, and she was alone in the house, refused him admittance.

The young poet fixed his eyes earnestly on her face for some time in silence, then slowly turning round left the house, and walked towards a small grove of trees just opposite. There he stood for a few moments resting against a tree, and facing the house as if to take one last vengeful or admiring glance, then went his way without once turning round.

The young girl had been watching him from the windows, and the moment he moved she passed out of the door like one in a dream, and followed him slowly, step by step, down the avenue. The maids grew alarmed, and called to her father, who ran out and shouted loudly for her to stop, but she never turned nor seemed to heed. The young man, however, looked round, and seeing the whole family in pursuit, quickened his pace, first glancing fixedly at the girl for a moment. Immediately she sprang towards him, and they were both almost out of sight, when one of the maids espied a piece of paper tied to a branch of the tree where the poet had rested. From curiosity she took it down, and the moment the knot was untied, the farmer's daughter suddenly stopped, became quite still, and when her father came up she allowed him to lead her back to the house without resistance.

When questioned, she said that she felt herself drawn by an invisible force to follow the young stranger wherever he might lead, and that she would have followed him through the world, for her life seemed to be bound up in his; she had no will to resist, and was conscious of nothing else but his presence. Suddenly, however, the spell was broken, and then she heard her father's voice, and knew how strangely she had acted. At the same time the power of the young man over her vanished, and the impulse to follow him was no longer in her heart.

The paper, on being opened, was found to contain five mysterious words written in blood, and in this order:

> Sator.
> Arepo.
> Tenet.
> Opera.
> Rotas.

These letters are so arranged that read in any way, right to left, left to right, up or down, the same words are produced; and when written in blood with a pen made of an eagle's feather, they form a charm which no woman (it is said) can resist; but the incredulous reader can easily test the truth of this assertion for himself.

The Poet's Malediction

THE imprecations of the poets had often also a mysterious and fatal effect.

King Breas, the pagan monarch, was a fierce, cruel, and niggardly man, who was therefore very unpopular with the people, who hate the cold heart and the grudging hand.

Amongst others who suffered by the king's inhospitality, was the renowned Carbury the poet, son of Eodain, the great poetess of the Tuatha-de-Danann race; she who chanted the song of victory when her people conquered the Firbolgs, on the plains of Moytura; and the stone that she stood on, during the battle, in sight of all the warriors, is still existing, and is pointed out as the stone of Eodain, the poetess, with great reverence, even to this day.

It was her son, Carbury the poet, who was held in such high honor by the nation that King Breas invited him to his court, in order that he might pronounce a powerful malediction over the enemy with whom he was then at war.

Carbury came on the royal summons, but in place of being treated with the distinction due to his high rank, he was lodged and fed so meanly that the soul of the poet raged with wrath; for the king gave him for lodgement only a small stone cell without fire or a bed; and for food he had only three cakes of meal without any flesh meat or sauce, and no wine was given him, such wine as is fit to light up the poet's soul before the divine mystic spirit of song can awake in its power within him. So very early the next morning, the poet rose up and departed, with much rage in his heart. But as he passed the king's house he stopped, and in place of a blessing, pronounced a terrible malediction over Breas and his race, which can still be found in the ancient books of Ireland, commencing thus:

> "Without fire, without bed, on the surface of the floor!
> Without meat, without fowl, on the surface of the dish.

Three little dishes and no flesh thereon,
A cell without bed, a dish without meat, a cup without wine,
Are these fit offerings from a king to a poet?
May the king and his race be three times accursed forever
        and forever!"

Immediately three large blisters rose on the king's forehead, and remained there as a sign and mark of the poet's vengeance.

And from that day forth to his death, which happened not long after, the reign of Breas was a time of sore trouble and disaster, for he was three times defeated by his enemies, and from care and sorrow a grievous disease fell on him; for though hungry he could not swallow any food; and though all the meat and wine of the best was set before him, yet his throat seemed closed, and though raging with hunger yet not a morsel could pass his lips; and so he died miserably, starved in the midst of plenty, and accursed in all things by the power and malediction of the angry poet.

The Poet and the King

Nuadhé, the celebrated poet, is remembered in history by a memorable exercise of his malefic power, and the punishment that fell on him in consequence; for Heaven is just, and even a bard cannot escape the penalty due for sin.

Nuadhé was nephew to Caer, the king of Connaught, who reared him with all kindness and gentleness as his own son. But by an evil fate the wife of Caer the king loved the young man; and she gave him a silver apple in proof of her love, and further promised him the kingdom and herself if he could overthrow Caer and make the people depose him from the sovranty.

"How can I do this?" answered Nuadhé, "for the king has ever been kind to me."

"Ask him for some gift," said the queen, "that he will refuse, and then put a blemish on him for punishment, that so he can be no longer king"; for no one with a blemish was ever suffered to reign in Erin.

"But he refuses me nothing," answered Nuadhé.

"Try him," said the queen. "Ask of him the dagger he brought from Alba, for he is under a vow never to part with it."

So Nuadhé went to him, and asked for the dagger that came out of Alba as a gift.

"Woe is me!" said the king. "This I cannot grant; for I am under a solemn vow never to part with it, or give it to another."

Then the poet by his power made a satire on him, and this was the form of the imprecation—

> "Evil death, and a short life
> Be on Caer the king!
> Let the spears of battle wound him,
> Under earth, under ramparts, under stones,
> Let the malediction be on him!"

And when Caer rose up in the morning he put his hand to his

face and found it was disfigured with three blisters, a white, a red, and a green. And when he saw the blemish he fled away filled with fear that any man should see him, and took refuge in a fort with one of his faithful servants, and no one knew where he lay hid.

So Nuadhé took the kingdom and held it for a year, and had the queen to wife. But then grievous to him was the fate of Caer, and he set forth to search for him.

And he was seated in the king's own royal chariot, with the king's wife beside him, and the king's greyhound at his feet, and all the people wondered at the beauty of the charioteer.

Now Caer was in the fort where he had found shelter, and when he saw them coming he said—

"Who is this that is seated in my chariot in the place of the champion, and driving my steeds?"

But when he saw that it was Nuadhé he fled away and hid himself for shame.

Then Nuadhé drove into the fort in the king's chariot, and loosed the dogs to pursue Caer. And they found him hid under the flagstone behind the rock even where the dogs tracked him. And Caer fell down dead from shame on beholding Nuadhé, and the rock where he fell flamed up and shivered into fragments, and a splinter leaped up high as a man, and struck Nuadhé on the eyes, and blinded him for life. Such was the punishment decreed, and just and right was the vengeance of God upon the sin of the poet.

Seanchan the Bard and the King of the Cats

In ancient Ireland men of learning were esteemed beyond all other classes; all the great ollaves and professors and poets held the very highest social position, and took precedence of the nobles, and ranked next to royalty. The leading men amongst them lived luxuriously in the great Bardic House; and when they went abroad through the country they travelled with a train of minor bards, fifty or more, and were entertained free of cost by the kings and chiefs, who considered themselves highly honoured by the presence of so distinguished a company at their court. If the receptions were splendid and costly, the praise of the entertainer was chanted by all the poets at the feast; but if any slight were offered, such stinging satire was poured forth in such bitter odes that many declared they would sooner die than incur the anger of the poets or be made the subject of their scathing satire.

All the learned men and professors, the ollaves of music, poetry, oratory, and of the arts and sciences generally, formed a great Bardic Association, who elected their own president, with the title of Chief Poet of all Ireland, and they also elected chief poets for each of the provinces. Learned women, likewise, and poetesses, were included in the Bardic Association, with distinct and recognized privileges, both as to revenue and costly apparel. Legal enactments even were made respecting the number of colors allowed to be worn in their mantles— the poet being allowed six colors, and the poetess five in her robe and mantle; the number of colors being a distinct recognition and visible sign of rank, and therefore very highly esteemed. But, in time, as a consequence of their many and great privileges, the pride and insolence of the learned class, the ollamhs, poets, and poetesses, became so insufferable, that even the kings trembled before them.

There is an amusing legend preserved in Ossianic tradition of the encounter between Seanchan, the celebrated chief poet of Ireland, and the King of all the Cats, who dwelt in a cave near Clonmacnoise.

When Seanchan, the renowned Bard, was made *Ard-Filé,* or Chief Poet of Ireland, Guaire, the king of Connaught, to do him honor, made a great feast for him and the whole Bardic Association. And all the professors went to the king's house, the great ollaves of poetry and history and music, and of the arts and sciences; and the learned, aged females, Grug and Grag and Grangait; and all the chief poets and poetesses of Ireland, an amazing number. But Guaire the king entertained them all splendidly, so that the ancient pathway to his palace is still called "The Road of the Dishes."

And each day he asked, "How fares it with my noble guests?" But they were all discontented, and wanted things he could not get for them. So he was very sorrowful, and prayed to God to be delivered from "the learned men and women, a vexatious class."

Still the feast went on for three days and three nights. And they drank and made merry. And the whole Bardic Association entertained the nobles with the choicest music and professional accomplishments.

But Seanchan sulked and would neither eat nor drink, for he was jealous of the nobles of Connaught. And when he saw how much they consumed of the best meats and wine, he declared he would taste no food till they and their servants were all sent away out of the house.

And when Guaire asked him again, "How fares my noble guest, and this great and excellent people?" Seanchan answered, "I have never had worse days, nor worse nights, nor worse dinners in my life." And he ate nothing for three whole days.

Then the king was sorely grieved that the whole Bardic Association should be feasting and drinking while Seanchan, the chief poet of Erin, was fasting and weak. So he sent his favorite serving-man, a person of mild manners and cleanliness, to offer special dishes to the bard.

"Take them away," said Seanchan; "I'll have none of them."

"And why, oh, Royal Bard?" asked the servitor.

"Because thou art an uncomely youth," answered Seanchan. "Thy grandfather was chip-nailed—I have seen him; I shall eat no food from thy hands."

Then the king called a beautiful maiden to him, his foster daughter, and said, "Lady, bring thou this wheaten cake and this dish of salmon to the illustrious poet, and serve him thyself." So the maiden went.

But when Seanchan saw her he asked: "Who sent thee hither, and why hast thou brought me food?"

"My lord the king sent me, oh, Royal Bard," she answered, "because I am comely to look upon, and he bade me serve thee with food myself."

"Take it away," said Seanchan. "Thou art an unseemly girl, I know of none more ugly. I have seen thy grandmother; she sat on a wall one day and pointed out the way with her hand to some travelling lepers. How could I touch thy food?" So the maiden went away in sorrow.

And then Guaire the king was indeed angry, and he exclaimed, "My malediction on the mouth that uttered that! May the kiss of a leper be on Seanchan's lips before he dies!"

Now there was a young serving-girl there, and she said to Seanchan, "There is a hen's egg in the place, my lord. May I bring it to thee, oh, Chief Bard?"

"It will suffice," said Seanchan. "Bring it that I may eat."

But when she went to look for it, behold the egg was gone.

"Thou hast eaten it," said the bard, in wrath.

"Not so, my lord," she answered; "but the mice, the nimble race, have carried it away."

"Then I will satirize them in a poem," said Seanchan; and forthwith he chanted so bitter a satire against them that ten mice fell dead at once in his presence.

"'Tis well," said Seanchan; "but the cat is the one most to blame, for it was her duty to suppress the mice. Therefore I shall satirize the tribe of the cats, and their chief lord, Irusan, son of Arusan. For I know where he lives with his wife Spit-Fire, and his daughter Sharp-Tooth, with her brothers, the Purrer and the Growler. But I shall begin with Irusan himself, for he is king, and answerable for all the cats."

And he said, "Irusan, monster of claws, who strikes at the mouse, but lets it go; weakest of cats. The otter did well who bit off the tips of thy progenitor's ears, so that every cat since is jagged-eared. Let thy tail hang down; it is right, for the mouse jeers at thee."

Now Irusan heard these words in his cave, and he said to his daughter, Sharp-Tooth: "Seanchan has satirized me, but I will be avenged."

"Nay, father," she said, "bring him here alive, that we may all take our revenge."

"I shall go then and bring him," said Irusan; "so send thy brothers after me."

Now when it was told to Seanchan that the King of the Cats was on his way to come and kill him, he was timorous, and besought Guaire and all the nobles to stand by and protect him. And before long a vibrating, impressive, impetuous sound was heard, like a raging tempest of fire in full blaze. And when the cat appeared he seemed to them of the size of a bullock; and this was his appearance—rapacious, panting, jagged-eared, snub-nosed, sharp-toothed, nimble, angry, vindictive, glare-eyed, terrible, sharp-clawed. Such was his similitude. But he passed on amongst them, not minding till he came to Seanchan; and him he seized by the arm and jerked him up on his back, and made off the way he came before anyone could touch him; for he had no other object in view but to get hold of the poet.

Now Seanchan, being in evil plight, had recourse to flattery. "Oh, Irusan," he exclaimed, "how truly splendid thou art, such running, such leaps, such strength, and such agility! But what evil have I done, oh, Irusan, son of Arusan? spare me, I entreat. I invoke the saints between thee and me, oh, great King of the Cats."

But not a bit did the cat let go his hold for all this fine talk, but went straight on to Clonmacnoise, where there was a forge; and St. Kieran happened to be there standing at the door.

"What!" exclaimed the saint; "is that the Chief Bard of Erin on the back of a cat? Has Guaire's hospitality ended in this?" And he ran for a red-hot bar of iron that was in the furnace, and struck the cat on the side with it, so that the iron passed through him, and he fell down lifeless.

"Now my curse on the hand that gave that blow!" said the bard, when he got upon his feet.

"And wherefore?" asked St. Kieran.

"Because," answered Seanchan, "I would rather Irusan had killed me, and eaten me every bit, that so I might bring disgrace on Guaire for the bad food he gave me; for it was all owing to his wretched dinners that I got into this plight."

And when all the other kings heard of Seanchan's misfortunes, they sent to beg he would visit their courts. But he would have neither kiss nor welcome from them, and went on his way to the bardic mansion, where the best of good living was always to be had. And ever after the kings were afraid to offend Seanchan.

So as long as he lived he had the chief place at the feast, and all the nobles there were made to sit below him, and Seanchan was content. And in time he and Guaire were reconciled; and Seanchan and all the ollamhs, and the whole Bardic Association, were feasted by the king for thirty days in noble style, and had the choicest of viands and the best of French wines to drink, served in goblets of silver. And in return for his splendid hospitality the Bardic Association decreed, unanimously, a vote of thanks to the king. And they praised him in poems as "Guaire the Generous," by which name he was ever after known in history, for the words of the poet are immortal.

9.
MURDER AND
MAYHEM

St. Brendan's Well and the Murderer

THE Well of St. Brendan, in High Island, has great virtue, but the miraculous power of the water is lost should a thief or a murderer drink of it.

Now a cruel murder had been committed on the mainland, and the priest notified the people that if the murderer tried to conceal himself in the island no one should harbor him or give him food or drink. It happened at that time there was a woman of the island afflicted with pains in her limbs, and she went to the Holy Well to make the stations and say the prayers, and so get cured. But many a day passed and still she got no better, though she went round and round the well on her knees, and recited the paters and aves as she was told.

Then she went to the priest and told him the story, and he perceived at once that the well had been polluted by the touch of someone who had committed a crime. So he bade the woman bring him a bottle of the water, and she did as he desired. Then having received the water, he poured it out, and breathed on it three times in the name of the Trinity; when, lo! the water turned into blood.

"Here is the evil," cried the priest. "A murderer has washed his hands in the well."

He then ordered her to make a fire in a circle, which she did, and he pronounced some words over it; and a mist rose up with the form of a spirit in the midst, holding a man by the arm.

"Behold the murderer," said the spirit; and when the woman looked on him she shrieked, "It is my son! My son!" and she fainted.

For the year before her son had gone to live on the mainland, and there, unknown to his mother, he had committed the dreadful murder for which the vengeance of God lay on him. And when she came to herself the spirit of the murderer was still there.

"Oh, my Lord! Let him go, let him go!" she cried.

"You wretched woman!" answered the priest. "How dare you interpose between God and vengeance. This is but the shadowy form of your son; but before night he shall be in the hands of the law, and justice shall be done."

Then the forms and the mist melted away, and the woman departed in tears, and not long after she died of a broken heart. But the well from that time regained all its miraculous powers, and the fame of its cures spread far and wide through all the islands.

Sheela-na-Skean

THERE is an old ruin of a farmhouse in the County Cork, near Fermoy, that has an evil reputation, and no one would build it up or inhabit it.

Years and years ago a rich farmer lived in the old farmhouse. He was reputed to have hoards of gold hid away in his sleeping-room. Some said he never slept without a sack of gold being laid under his pillow. However, one night he was found cruelly murdered, and all the gold in the house was missing except a few pieces stained with blood that had evidently been dropped by the murderers in their flight.

The old man at the time was living quite alone. His wife was dead, and his only son was away in a distant part of the country. But on news of the murder the son returned, and a close investigation was made. Suspicion finally fell on the housekeeper and a lover she used to bring to the house. They were arrested in consequence and brought to trial. The housekeeper, *Sheela-na-Skean*, or Sheela of the Knife, as she was called afterwards, was a dark, fierce, powerful woman, noted for her violent and vindictive temper. The lover was a weak, cowardly fellow, who at the last turned evidence to save his life. He had taken no part, he said, in the actual murder, though he had helped Sheela to remove and bury the gold. According to his story, Sheela entered the old man's room at night, and taking a sharp, short sword that always hung at the head of his bed, she stabbed him fiercely over and over till not a breath of life was left. Then, calling her lover, she ransacked the room, and found quantities of golden guineas, which they put in a bag and carried out to the field, where they buried it in a safe spot, known only to themselves; but this place neither Sheela nor the lover would reveal unless they received a pardon.

The murder, however, was too atrocious for pardons, and Sheela was hung amid the howlings and execrations of the people. But she remained fierce and defiant to the last, still refusing obstinately to reveal the place where the money was buried.

The lover, meanwhile, had died in prison from fright, for after sentence was pronounced, he fell down in a fit, from which he never recovered. So the secret of the gold died with them.

After this the son came to live in the place; and the tradition of the hidden gold was still kept alive in the family, but all efforts to find it proved useless.

Now a strange thing happened. The farmer dreamed for three nights in succession that if he went at midnight to an old ruined castle in the neighborhood, he would hear words that might tell him the secret of the gold; but he must go alone. So after the third dream the farmer resolved to do as he was ordered, and he went forth at midnight to the place indicated. His two sons, grown-up young men, anxiously awaited his return. And about an hour after midnight the father came home pale as a ghost, haggard and trembling. They helped him to his bed, and after a little he was able to tell them his adventures. He said, on reaching the old ruin he leaned up straight against the wall, and waited for the promised words in silence. Then a breath seemed to pass over his face, and he heard a low voice whispering in his ear, "If you want to find the bag of gold, take out the third stone."

"But here," said the farmer mournfully, "the voice stopped before the place was named where the gold lay; for at that instant a terrific screech was heard, and the ghost of Sheela appeared gigantic and terrible; her hands dripping with blood, and her eyes flaming fire; and she rushed to attack me, brandishing a short, sharp sword round her head, the very same, perhaps, with which she had committed the murder. At sight of this awful apparition I fled homeward, Sheela still pursuing me with leaps and yells till I reached the boundary of the castle grounds, when she sank into the earth and disappeared. But," continued the farmer, "I am certain, from the voice, that the bag of gold lies hid under the third stone in—"

He could say no more, for at that instant the door of the bedroom was violently flung open, as if by a strong storm wind, the candle was blown out, and the unfortunate man was lifted from

his bed by invisible hands, and dashed upon the floor with a terrible crash. In the darkness the young men could hear the groans, but they saw no one.

When the candle was relit they went over to help their father, but found he was already dead, with a black mark round his throat as if from strangulation by a powerful hand. So the secret of the gold remained still undiscovered.

After the funeral was over, and all affairs settled, the brothers agreed that they would still search for the gold in the old ruins of the castle, undeterred by the apparition of the terrible Sheela. So on a certain midnight they set forth with spades and big sticks for defense, and proceeded to examine every third stone in the huge walls, to the height of a man from the ground, seeking some secret mark or sign by which, perhaps, the true stone might be discovered. But as they worked, a thin blue light suddenly appeared at some distance in the inner court of the castle, and by it stood the ghost of their father, pointing with his outstretched hand to a certain stone in the wall. Now, they thought, that must certainly be the spot where the gold is hid; and they rushed on; but before they could reach the place, the terrible form of Sheela appeared, more awful than words could describe, clothed in white, and with a circle of flame round her head. And she seized the ghost with her gory hands, and dragged him away with horrible yells and imprecations. And far off in the darkness they could hear the fight going on, and the yells of Sheela as she pursued the ghost.

"Now," said the young men, "let us work while they are fighting"; and they worked away at the third stone from the end, where the blue light had rested—a large flat stone, but easily lifted; and when they had rolled it away from the place, there underneath lay a huge bag of bright golden guineas. And as they raised it up from the earth, a terrific unearthly din was heard in the distance, and a shrill scream rang on the air. Then a rush of the wind came by them and the blue light vanished, but they heeded nothing, only lifted the bag from the clay, and carried it away with them through the darkness and storm. And the yells seemed to pursue them till they reached the boundary of the castle grounds. Then all was still; and they traversed the rest of the way in peace, and reached home safely.

From that time the ghost of *Sheela-na-Skean* ceased to haunt the castle, but lamenting and cries used sometimes to be heard at night in and around the old farmhouse; so the brothers pulled it down and left it a ruin, and built a handsome residence with some of their treasure; for now they had plenty of gold, and they lived happily and prospered ever after, with all their family and possessions. And on the spot where the gold was found they erected a cross, in memory of their father, to whom they owed all their wealth, and through whom this prosperity had come; for by him the evil spirit of *Sheela-na-Skean* was conquered at last, and the gold restored to the family of the murdered farmer.

A Woman's Curse

THERE was a woman of the Island of Innis-Sark who was determined to take revenge on a man because he called her by an evil name. So she went to the Saints' Well, and, kneeling down, she took some of the water and poured it on the ground in the name of the devil, saying, "So may my enemy be poured out like water, and lie helpless on the earth!" Then she went round the well backwards on her knees, and at each station she cast a stone in the name of the devil, and said, "So may the curse fall on him, and the power of the devil crush him!" After this she returned home.

Now the next morning there was a stiff breeze, and some of the men were afraid to go out fishing; but others said they would try their luck, and amongst them was the man on whom the curse rested. But they had not gone far from land when the boat was capsized by a heavy squall. The fishermen, however, saved themselves by swimming to shore; all except the man on whom the curse rested, and he sank like lead to the bottom, and the waves covered him, and he was drowned.

When the woman heard of the fate that had befallen her enemy, she ran to the beach and clapped her hands with joy and exulted. And as she stood there laughing with strange and horrid mirth, the corpse of the man she had cursed slowly rose up from the sea, and came drifting towards her till it lay almost at her very feet. On this she stooped down to feast her eyes on the sight of the dead man, when suddenly a storm of wind screamed past her, and hurled her from the point of rock where she stood. And when the people ran in all haste to help, no trace of her body could be seen. The woman and the corpse of the man she had cursed disappeared together under the waves, and were never seen again from that time forth.

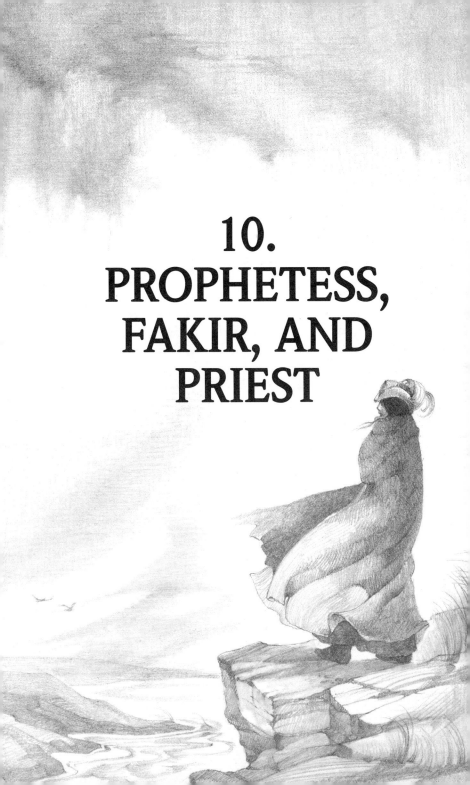

10.
PROPHETESS, FAKIR, AND PRIEST

Queen Maeve

MAEVE , the great queen of Connaught, holds a distinguished place in Bardic Legends. When she went to battle, it is said, she rode in an open car, accompanied by four chariots—one before, another behind, and one on each side—so that the golden assion on her head and her royal robes should not be defiled by the dust of the horses' feet, or the foam of the fiery steeds; for all the sovereigns of Ireland sat crowned with a diadem in battle, as they drove in their war-chariots, as well as in the festal and the public assemblies.

The Bardic Legends tell of a form that appeared to Maeve, queen of Connaught, on the eve of battle. Suddenly there stood before the queen's chariot a tall and beautiful woman. She wore a green robe clasped with a golden bodkin, a golden fillet on her head, and seven braids for the Dead of bright gold were in her hand. Her skin was white as snow that falls in the night; her teeth were as pearls; her lips red as the berries of the mountain ash; her golden hair fell to the ground; and her voice was sweet as the golden harp-string when touched by a skillful hand.

"Who art thou, O woman?" asked the queen, in astonishment.

"I am Feithlinn, the fairy prophetess of the Rath of Cruachan," she answered.

"'Tis well, O Feithlinn the prophetess," said Maeve; "but what dost thou foresee concerning our hosts?"

"I foresee bloodshed; I foresee power; I foresee defeat!" answered the prophetess.

"My couriers have brought me good tidings!" said the queen; "my army is strong, my warriors are well prepared. But speak the truth, O prophetess; for my soul knows no fear."

"I foresee bloodshed; I foresee victory!" answered the prophetess the second time.

"But I have nothing to fear from the Ultonians," said the queen, "for my couriers have arrived, and my enemies are under dread. Yet, speak the truth, O prophetess, that our hosts may know it."

"I foresee bloodshed; I foresee conquest; I foresee *death!*" answered the prophetess, for the third time.

"To me then it belongs not, thy prophecy of evil," replied the queen, in anger.

"Be it thine, and on thy own head."

And even as she spoke the prophet maiden disappeared, and the queen saw her no more.

But it so happened that, some time afterwards, Queen Maeve was cruelly slain by her own kinsman, at Lough Rea by the Shannon, to avenge the assistance she had given in war to the king of Ulster. There is an island in the lake where is shown the spot where the great queen was slain, and which is still known to the people as "the Stone of the Dead Queen."

The Irish Fakir

MANY of the professional prayer-men, or Fakirs, manage to obtain gifts and contributions and all sorts of excellent things in exchange for their prayers from the rich farmers and young girls, to whom they promise good luck, and perhaps also a lover who will be handsome and young.

These Irish Fakirs, or sacred fraternity of beggars, lead a pleasant, thoroughly idle life. They carry a wallet and a staff, and being looked on as holy men endowed with strange spiritual gifts, they are entirely supported by the voluntary gifts of the people, who firmly believe in the mysterious efficacy of their prayers and blessings and prognostics of luck.

One of these Fakirs towards the end of his life was glad to find shelter in the poor-house. He was then eighty years of age, but a tall, erect old man, with flowing white beard and hair, keen eyes, and of the most venerable aspect.

A gentleman who saw him there, being much struck with his dignified and remarkable appearance, induced him to tell the story of his life, which was marked by several strange and curious incidents.

He said he was a farmer's son, but from his earliest youth hated work, and only liked to spend the long summer day lying on the grass gazing up into the clouds dreaming and thinking where they were all sailing to, and longing to float away with them to other lands.

Meanwhile his father raged and swore and beat him, often cruelly, because he would not work. But all the same, he could not bring himself to be digging from morning to night, and herding cattle, and keeping company only with laborers. So when he was about twenty he formed a plan to run away; for, he thought, if the stupid old Fakirs who are lame and blind and deaf find people ready to support them, all for nothing, might not he have a better chance for getting board and lodging without work, since he had youth and health and could tell them stories to no end of the great old ancient times.

So one night he quitted his father's house secretly, and went forth on his travels into the wide world, only to meet bitter disappointment and rude repulse, for the farmers would have nothing to say to him, nor the farmers' wives. Everyone eyed him with suspicion. "Why," they said, "should a great stalwart young fellow over six feet high go about the country begging? He is a tramp and means no good." And they chased him away from their grounds.

Then he thought he would disguise himself as a regular Fakir; so he got a long cloak, and took a wallet and a staff, and hid his raven black hair under a close skull cap, and tried to look as old as he could.

But the regular Fakirs soon found him out, and their spite and rage was great, for all of them were either lame of a leg or blind of an eye, and they said, "Why should this great broad-shouldered young fellow with black eyes come and take away our chances of living, when he ought to be able to work and earn enough to keep himself without robbing us of our just rights?" And they grumbled and snarled at him like so many dogs, and set people to spy on him and watch him.

Still he was determined to try his luck on every side: so he went to all the stations round about and prayed louder and faster than any pilgrim or Fakir amongst the whole lot.

But wherever he went, he saw a horrible old hag forever following him. Her head was wrapped up in an old red shawl, and nothing was seen of her face except two eyes, that glared on him like coals of fire whichever way he turned. And now, in truth, his life became miserable to him because of this loathsome hag. So he went from station to station to escape her; but still she followed him, and the sound of her stick on the ground was ever after him like the hammering of a nail into his coffin, for he felt sure he would die of the torment and horror.

At last he thought he would try *Tobar-Breda* for his next station, as it was several miles off and she might not be able to follow him so far. So he went, and not a sign of her was to be seen upon the road. This rejoiced his heart, and he kneeled down at the well and was saying his prayers louder and faster than ever when he looked up, and there, kneeling right opposite to him at the other side of the road, was the detestable old witch. But she took no notice of him, only went on saying her prayers and telling her beads as if no one were by.

Presently, however, she stooped down to wash her face in the well, and, as she threw up the water with her hands, she let the red shawl slip down over her shoulders, and then the young man beheld to his astonishment a beautiful young girl before him with a complexion like the lily and the rose, and soft brown hair falling in showers of curls over her snow-white neck.

He had only a glimpse for a moment while she cast the water in her face, and then she drew the red shawl again over her head and shoulders and was the old hag once more that had filled him with horror. But that one glimpse was enough to make his heart faint with love; and now for the first time she turned her burning eyes full on him, and kept them fixed until he seemed to swoon away in an ecstasy of happiness, and knew nothing more till he found her seated beside him, holding his hand in hers, and still looking intently on his face with her glittering eyes.

"Come away," she whispered. "Follow me. We must leave this crowd of pilgrims. I have much to say to you."

So he rose up, and they went away together to a secluded spot, far from the noise and tumult of the station. Then she threw off the shawl, and took the bandage from her face, and said, "Look on me. Can you love me? I have followed you day by day for love of you. Can you love me in return, and join your fate to mine? I have money enough for both, and I'll teach you the mysteries by which we can gain more."

And from that day forth they two travelled together all over the country; and they practiced many strange mysteries and charms, for Elaine, his wife, was learned in all the secrets of herb lore. And the people paid them well for their help and knowledge, so that they never wanted anything, and lived like princes, though never an evil act was done by their hands, nor did a word of strife ever pass between them.

Thus they lived happily for many years, till an evil day came when Elaine was struck by sickness, and she died.

Then the soul of the man seemed to die with her, and all his knowledge left him, and sad and weary, and tired of all things, he finally came to end his days in the poor-house, old, poor, and broken-hearted. Yet still he had the bearing of one born for a higher destiny, and the noble dignity as of a discrowned king.

Such was the strange story told to the gentleman by the aged Fakir in the poor-house, a short time before his death.

The Doom

THERE was a young man of Innismore, named James Lynan, noted through all the island for his beauty and strength. Never a one could beat him at hunting or wrestling, and he was, besides, the best dancer in the whole townland. But he was bold and reckless, and ever foremost in all the wild wicked doings of the young fellows of the place.

One day he happened to be in chapel after one of these mad freaks, and the priest denounced him by name from the altar.

"James Lynan," he said, "remember my words; you will come to an ill end. The vengeance of God will fall on you for your wicked life; and by the power that is in me I denounce you as an evil liver and a limb of Satan, and accursed of all good men."

The young man turned pale, and fell on his knees before all the people, crying out bitterly, "Have mercy, have mercy; I repent, I repent," and he wept like a woman.

"Go now in peace," said the priest, "and strive to lead a new life, and I'll pray to God to save your soul."

From that day forth James Lynan changed his ways. He gave up drinking, and never a drop of spirits crossed his lips. And he began to attend to his farm and his business, in place of being at all the mad revels and dances and fairs and wakes in the island. Soon after he married a nice girl, a rich farmer's daughter, from the mainland, and they had four fine children, and all things prospered with him.

But the priest's words never left his mind, and he would suddenly turn pale and a shivering would come over him when the memory of the curse came upon him. Still he prospered, and his life was a model of sobriety and order.

One day he and his wife and their children were asked to the wedding of a friend about four miles off; and James Lynan rode to the place, the family going on their own car. At the wedding he was the life of the party as he always was; but never a drop of drink touched his lips. When evening came on, the family set out for the return home just as they had set out; the wife and children on the car, James Lynan riding his own horse. But when the wife arrived at home, she found her husband's horse standing at the gate riderless and quite still. They thought he might have fallen in a faint, and went back to search; when he was found down in a hollow not five perches from his own gate, lying quite insensible and his features distorted frightfully, as if seized while looking on some horrible vision.

They carried him in, but he never spoke. A doctor was sent for, who opened a vein, but no blood came. There he lay like a log, speechless as one dead. Amongst the crowd that gathered round was an old woman accounted very wise by the people.

"Send for the fairy doctor," she said; "he is struck."

So they sent off a boy on the fastest horse for the fairy man. He could not come himself, but he filled a bottle with a potion. Then he said, "Ride for your life; give him some of this to drink and sprinkle his face and hands also with it. But take care as you pass the lone bush on the round hill near the hollow, for the fairies are there and will hinder you if they can, and strive to break the bottle."

Then the fairy man blew into the mouth and the eyes and the nostrils of the horse, and turned him round three times on the road and rubbed the dust off his hoofs.

"Now go," he said to the boy; "go and never look behind you, no matter what you hear."

So the boy went like the wind, having placed the bottle safely in his pocket; and when he came to the lone bush the horse started and gave such a jump that the bottle nearly fell, but the boy caught it in time and held it safe and rode on. Then he heard a cluttering of feet behind him, as of men in pursuit; but he never turned or looked, for he knew it was the fairies who were after him. And shrill voices cried to him, "Ride fast, ride fast, for the spell is cast!" Still he never turned round, but rode on, and never let go his hold of the fairy draught till he stopped at his master's door, and handed the potion to the poor sorrowing wife. And she gave of it to the sick man to drink, and sprinkled his face and hands, after which he fell into a deep sleep. But when he woke up, though he knew everyone around him, the power of speech was gone from him; and from that time to his death, which happened soon after, he never uttered word more.

So the doom of the priest was fulfilled—evil was his youth and evil was his fate, and sorrow and death found him at last, for the doom of the priest is as the word of God.

The Priest's Soul

In former days there were great schools in Ireland where every sort of learning was taught to the people, and even the poorest had more knowledge at that time than many a gentleman has now. But as to the priests, their learning was above all, so that the fame of Ireland went over the whole world, and many kings from foreign lands used to send their sons all the way to Ireland to be brought up in the Irish schools.

There was a little boy learning at one of the great schools who was a wonder to everyone for his cleverness. His parents were only laboring people, and of course very poor; but young as he was, and poor as he was, no king's or lord's son could come up to him in learning. Even the masters were put to shame, for when they were trying to teach him he would tell them something they never heard of before, and show them their ignorance. One of his great triumphs was in argument; and he would go on till he proved to you that black was white, and then when you gave in, for no one could beat him in talk, he would turn round and show you that white was black, or maybe that there was no color at all in the world. When he grew up, his poor father and mother were so proud of him that they resolved to make him a priest, which they did at last, though they nearly starved themselves to get the money. Well, such another learned man was not in Ireland, and he was as great in argument as ever, so that no one could stand before him. Even the bishops tried to talk to him, but he showed them at once they knew nothing at all.

Now there were no schoolmasters in those times but it was the priests taught the people; and as this man was the cleverest in Ireland all the foreign kings sent their sons to him as long as he had house-room to give them. So he grew very proud, and began to forget how low he had been, and worst of all, even to forget God, who had made him what he was. And the pride of arguing got hold of him, so that from one thing to another he went on to prove that there was no Purgatory, and then no Hell, and then no Heaven, and then no God; and at last that men had no souls, but were no more than a dog or a cow, and when they died there was an end of them.

"Who ever saw a soul?" he would say. "If you can show me one, I will believe."

No one could make any answer to this; and at last they all came to believe that as there was no other world, everyone might do what they liked in this; the priest setting the example, for he took a beautiful young girl to wife. But as no priest or bishop in the whole land could be got to marry them, he was obliged to read the service over for himself. It was a great scandal, yet no one dared to say a word, for all the kings' sons were on his side, and would have slaughtered anyone who tried to prevent his wicked goings-on. Poor boys! they all believed in him, and thought every word he said was the truth. In this way his notions began to spread about, and the whole world was going to the bad, when one night an angel came down from Heaven, and told the priest he had but twenty-four hours to live. He began to tremble, and asked for a little more time.

But the angel was stiff, and told him that could not be. "What do you want time for, you sinner?" he asked.

"Oh, sir, have pity on my poor soul!" urged the priest.

"Oh, ho! You have a soul, then," said the angel. "Pray, how did you find that out?"

"It has been fluttering in me ever since you appeared," answered the priest. "What a fool I was not to think of it before!"

"A fool indeed," said the angel. "What good was all your learning, when it could not tell you that you had a soul?"

"Ah, my lord," said the priest, "if I am to die, tell me how soon I may be in Heaven?"

"Never," replied the angel. "You denied there was a Heaven."

"Then, my lord, may I go to Purgatory?"

"You denied Purgatory also; you must go straight to Hell," said the angel.

"But, my lord, I denied Hell also," answered the priest, "so you can't send me there either."

The angel was a little puzzled.

"Well," said he, "I'll tell you what I can do for you. You may

either live now on earth for a hundred years enjoying every pleasure, and then be cast into Hell forever; or you may die in twenty-
four hours in the most horrible torments, and pass through Purgatory, there to remain till the Day of Judgment, if only you can
find some one person that believes, and through his belief mercy
will be vouchsafed to you and your soul will be saved."

The priest did not take five minutes to make up his mind.

"I will have death in the twenty-four hours," he said, "so that
my soul may be saved at last."

On this the angel gave him directions as to what he was to do,
and left him.

Then, immediately, the priest entered the large room where
all his scholars and the kings' sons were seated, and called out to
them, "Now, tell me the truth, and let none fear to contradict
me. Tell me what is your belief. Have men souls?"

"Master," they answered, "once we believed that men had
souls; but, thanks to your teaching, we believe so no longer. There
is no Hell, and no Heaven, and no God. This is our belief, for it
is thus you taught us."

Then the priest grew pale with fear and cried out, "Listen! I
taught you a lie. There is a God, and man has an immortal soul.
I believe now all I denied before."

But the shouts of laughter that rose up drowned the priest's
voice, for they thought he was only trying them for argument.

"Prove it, master," they cried, "prove it. Who has ever seen
God? Who has ever seen the soul?"

And the room stirred with their laughter.

The priest stood up to answer them, but no word could he
utter; all his eloquence, all his powers of argument had gone from
him, and he could do nothing but wring his hands and cry out,
"There is a God! there is a God! Lord have mercy on my soul!"

And they all began to mock him, and repeat his own words
that he had taught them: "Show him to us; show us your God."

And he fled from them groaning with agony, for he saw that
none believed, and how then could his soul be saved?

But he thought next of his wife. "She will believe," he said to
himself. "Women never give up God."

And he went to her; but she told him that she believed only what he taught her, and that a good wife should believe in her husband first, and before and above all things in heaven or earth.

Then despair came on him, and he rushed from the house and began to ask everyone he met if they believed. But the same answer came from one and all: "We believe only what you have taught us," for his doctrines had spread far and wide through the county.

Then he grew half mad with fear, for the hours were passing. And he flung himself down on the ground in a lonesome spot, and wept and groaned in terror, for the time was coming fast when he must die.

Just then a little child came by. "God save you kindly," said the child to him.

The priest started up. "Child, do you believe in God?" he asked.

"I have come from a far country to learn about Him," said the child. "Will your honor direct me to the best school that they have in these parts?"

"The best school and the best teacher is close by," said the priest, and he named himself.

"Oh, not to that man," answered the child, "for I am told he denies God, and Heaven, and Hell, and even that man has a soul, because we can't see it; but I would soon put him down."

The priest looked at him earnestly. "How?" he inquired.

"Why," said the child, "I would ask him if he believed he had life to show me his life."

"But he could not do that, my child," said the priest. "Life cannot be seen; we have it, but it is invisible."

"Then if we have life, though we cannot see it, we may also have a soul, though it is invisible," answered the child.

When the priest heard him speak these words, he fell down on his knees before him, weeping for joy, for now he knew his soul was safe; he had met at last one that believed. And he told the child his whole story: all his wickedness, and pride, and blasphemy against the great God; and how the angel had come to him and told him of the only way in which he could be saved, through the faith and prayers of someone who believed.

"Now then," he said to the child, "take this penknife and strike it into my breast, and go on stabbing the flesh until you see the paleness of death on my face. Then watch—for a living thing will soar up from my body as I die, and you will then know that my soul has ascended to the presence of God. And when you see this thing, make haste and run to my school and call on all my scholars to come and see that the soul of their master has left the body, and that all he taught them was a lie, for that there is a God who punishes sin, and a Heaven and a Hell, and that man has an immortal soul, destined for eternal happiness or misery."

"I will pray," said the child, "to have courage to do this work."

And he kneeled down and prayed. Then when he rose up he took the penknife and struck it into the priest's heart, and struck and struck again till all the flesh was lacerated; but still the priest lived though the agony was horrible, for he could not die until the twenty-four hours had expired. At last the agony seemed to cease, and the stillness of death settled on his face. Then the child, who was watching, saw a beautiful living creature, with four snow-white wings, mount from the dead man's body into the air and go fluttering round his head.

So he ran to bring the scholars; and when they saw it they all knew it was the soul of their master, and they watched with wonder and awe until it passed from sight into the clouds.

And this was the first butterfly that was ever seen in Ireland; and now all men know that the butterflies are the souls of the dead waiting for the moment when they may enter Purgatory, and so pass through torture to purification and peace.

But the schools of Ireland were quite deserted after that time, for people said, What is the use of going so far to learn when the wisest man in all Ireland did not know if he had a soul till he was near losing it; and was only saved at last through the simple belief of a little child?

Index

Angel, 122–124

Animals, legends of, 51–58

Apple, 94

Apples, A Spell of, 74–76

Ard-Filé, 97

Arusan, father of Irusan, 98

Athair-Luss, 30

Ballytowtas Castle, Legend of, 78–86

Bardic Association, 96–97, 101

Beggars, 81–82, 114

Boffin, 35

Boyne, 32

Breas, King, 92

Brendan, St., 103

Butterfly, the first in Ireland, 126

Butter Mystery, The, 69–70

Butter, spells over, 14, 71

Caer, king of Connaught, 94

Callan, Mary, 48–49

Carbury the Poet, 92

Cashel, 74

Castlerea, family of, 60–61

Cathal, king of Munster, 74–76

Cats, 83; King of the, 96–101; The Monstrous, 57–58

Cave Fairies, The, 21–25

Changeling, The, 26–27

Charm no woman can resist, 91

Chess, game of, 22

Christianity, 5

Clare, County, 42

Clonmacmoise, 96, 99

Coffin carriers, 18–20

Connaught, queen of, 112

Connemara, 87

Connor, farmer, 51–54; Hugh, 71–73

Cork, County, 105

Cows, 51–54

Cruachan, Rath of, 112

Curse, A Woman's, 110

Dairy, 69–70

Dance, The Fairy, 28–30

Dancing, 28–30, 41

Dark Horseman, The, 17–21

Daughter, farmer's, 90–91

Dead, 112; Hand, The, 14–15; Legends of the, 46–49; souls of the, 126

Death, Spirit of, 57–58

Dermot of Shark, 57–58

Doctors, 83; see Fairy doctor

Doom, The, 118–120

Druids, 24

Dublin, 61, 72, 81, 83

Eagle, 37

Edain, the fair, 22–25

Elaine, wife of the Fakir, 115–116

Elder-tree, 69–70, 74

Eodain, the poetess, 92

Evil Eye, 72–73, 77–79

Evil spells, 71–73

Fairies, 16–49, 55, 69

Fairy doctor, 69, 119

Fakir, 114–117

Farmer Punished, The, 32–35

Fascination by the glance, 90–91

Feithlinn, the prophetess, 112

Fenian Knights, The, 87–88

Fergus, king of Ulster, 74, 76

Fermoy, 105

Fionn Ma-Coul, 87–88

Firbolgs, 92

Fort of the Mantle, 44

Future, visions of the, 87–88

Galway, County, 78

Gander, 38

Ghost, 106–109

Giant, one-eyed, 87–88

Glance, fascination by the, 90–91

Goblet, 85

Gold, pot of, 60–64

Grag, 97

Grangait, 97

Growler, the, 98

Grug, 97

Guaire, king of Connaught, 97–101

Hand, dead, 14–15

Harp, 85

Hazel-tree, 25

Herbs, ring of, 46

High Island, 103

Horned Women, The, 7–11

Horns, 7–11, 86

Horseman, The Dark, 17–21

Horses, Phantom, 55–56

Innis-bo-finn, 35

Innis-Erk, 35

Innismore, 118

Innis-Sark, 37, 46, 110

Irusan, lord of the Cats, 98–101

Ivy, ground, 30

Joyce County, 12

Kathleen, 46–47

Kern of Querin, 42–45

Kieran, St., 99–101

Killeries, 87

Kittens, 83

Lady Witch, The, 12–13

Language, 5

Leaf, spell of the, 49

Leinster, king of, 33

Leprechauns, 59–64

Leydon, Mary, 71–73

Limerick, County, 90

Lios-na-fallainge, 44

Lipenshaw, fort of, 61

Lis-na-Keeran, 87

Little men, 37, 65–67

Lough Rea, 113

Lynan, James, 118–120

Ma-Coul, Fionn, 87–88
Maeve, Queen, 112–113
Magic spells, 68–88
Malediction, The Poet's, 92–93
Manna, gathering, 78–79
Mantle, Fort of the, 44
Mice, 98–99
Midar, 22–25
Milesians, 21
Milk, spells over, 71
Monuments, ancient, 5
Moon, 37–38
Moytura, plains of, 92
Munster, 22, 74–76
Murder and Mayhem, 102–110
Murderer, 103–104
Mythology, 5
November: Eve, 42; nights, 29, 41–45
Nowlan, Jemmy, 17–21
Nuadhe, the poet, 94–95
O'Connor, daughter of, 44–45
Oak tree, 85
Oghams, 24–25
Ollamhs, 5, 96, 101
Ollaves, 96–97
Oscar of the Lion Heart, 87–88
Osiris, 30
Ossianic tradition, 96
Otter, 98
Phadrig, 64–67
Phantom Horses, 55–56
Phouka, 64–67

Poet and the Farmer's Daughter, The, 90–91
Poets, 76, 89–101
Poet and the King, 94–95
Power of Poets 89–101
Prayer-men, 114
Prophecy, 112–113
Prophetess, Fakir, and Priest, 111–126
Purgatory, 122–126
Purrer, the, 98
Querin, County Clare, 42
Red-haired man, 18, 35–36
Ring, magic, 80–86
Ring of herbs, 46
Road of the Dishes, The, 97
Saints' Well, 110
Samhain, 42
Schools of Ireland, great, 121
Seanchan the Bard, 96–101
Shannon, 113
Shark Island, 35, 38, 41, 48, 57–58
Sharp-tooth, 98
Shaun-Mor, 37–41
Sheela-na-Skean, 105–109
Sheep, fleece of, 88
Slane, Ireland, 17
Slieve-namon, 11
Soul, The Priest's, 121–126

Spells, magic, 68–88
Spirit of the Well, 10–11
Spit-Fire, 98
St. Erk Island, 35
St. Kieran, 99–101
St. Brendan's Well and the Murderer, 103–104
Stolen Bride, The, 42–45
Stone of the Dead Queen, The, 113
Supernatural, 5
Superstition, 5
Tara, 22, 25
Thrift, 32
Thumb, chewing of, 87–88
Tobar-Breda, 115
Towtas, 78–86
Tricks, fairy, 16–30
Tuatha-de-Dananns, 21–25, 92
Ulster, king of, 113
Ulster, 74
Ultonians, 112
Vengeance, Fairy, 31–45
Well, St. Brendan's, 103
Well, Saints', 110
Western Isles, 28
Whale, 38
White Cow, Island of the, 35
Whitsuntide, 55, 56
Widow, The Wicked, 71–73
Wife-beating, 36
Witches, 7–15
Wolves, 51–54, 76